GOD'S ABSOLUTE LOVE
ABSOLUTE TRUTH

JOY MALOY

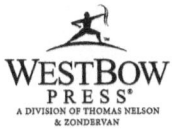

WestBow Press
A DIVISION OF THOMAS NELSON
& ZONDERVAN

Copyright © 2020 Joy Maloy.

All rights reserved. No part of this book may be used or reproduced by any means, graphic, electronic, or mechanical, including photocopying, recording, taping or by any information storage retrieval system without the written permission of the author except in the case of brief quotations embodied in critical articles and reviews.

Disclaimer: Author does not claim to interpret God's Holy Word, His Holy Spirit does that, and she is not giving professional advice in any way, just sharing some things she has seen in the Bible as a layperson. All that read this book should prayerfully read it, and check its accuracy by reading the Good Book, the Holy Bible for themselves.

WestBow Press books may be ordered through booksellers or by contacting:

WestBow Press
A Division of Thomas Nelson & Zondervan
1663 Liberty Drive
Bloomington, IN 47403
www.westbowpress.com
1 (866) 928-1240

Because of the dynamic nature of the Internet, any web addresses or links contained in this book may have changed since publication and may no longer be valid. The views expressed in this work are solely those of the author and do not necessarily reflect the views of the publisher, and the publisher hereby disclaims any responsibility for them.

Any people depicted in stock imagery provided by Getty Images are models, and such images are being used for illustrative purposes only.
Certain stock imagery © Getty Images.

ISBN: 978-1-9736-9458-8 (sc)
ISBN: 978-1-9736-9455-7 (e)

Print information available on the last page.

WestBow Press rev. date: 08/07/2020

Unless otherwise indicated, all Scripture is taken from the King James Version of the Bible.

Scripture marked (EXB) taken from The Expanded Bible. Copyright ©2011 by Thomas Nelson. Used by permission. All rights reserved.

Scripture quotations marked (NLT) are taken from the Holy Bible, New Living Translation, copyright ©1996, 2004, 2015 by Tyndale House Foundation. Used by permission of Tyndale House Publishers, a Division of Tyndale House Ministries, Carol Stream, Illinois 60188. All rights reserved.

Scripture quotations marked (NIV) are taken from the Holy Bible, New International Version®, NIV®. Copyright © 1973, 1978, 1984, 2011 by Biblica, Inc.® Used by permission of Zondervan. All rights reserved worldwide. www.zondervan.com The "NIV" and "New International Version" are trademarks registered in the United States Patent and Trademark Office by Biblica, Inc.®

Scripture marked (NKJV) taken from the New King James Version®. Copyright © 1982 by Thomas Nelson. Used by permission. All rights reserved.

Scripture quotations marked NLV are taken from the New Life Version, copyright © 1969 and 2003. Used by permission of Barbour Publishing, Inc., Uhrichsville, Ohio 44683. All rights reserved.

Scripture quotations marked (NASB) taken from the New American Standard Bible® (NASB), Copyright © 1960, 1962, 1963, 1968, 1971, 1972, 1973, 1975, 1977, 1995 by The Lockman Foundation Used by permission. www.Lockman.org

Scripture marked (ERV) taken from the Holy Bible: Easy-to-Read Version (ERV), International Edition © 2013, 2016 by Bible League International and used by permission.

Scripture quotations marked TPT are from The Passion Translation®. Copyright © 2017, 2018 by Passion & Fire Ministries, Inc. Used by permission. All rights reserved. ThePassionTranslation.com.

Scripture quotations marked (TLB) are taken from The Living Bible copyright © 1971. Used by permission of Tyndale House Publishers, a Division of Tyndale House Ministries, Carol Stream, Illinois 60188. All rights reserved.

Scripture quotations marked MSG are taken from THE MESSAGE, copyright © 1993, 2002, 2018 by Eugene H. Peterson. Used by permission of NavPress. All rights reserved. Represented by Tyndale House Publishers, a Division of Tyndale House Ministries.

Scripture quotations marked (ESV) are from the ESV® Bible (The Holy Bible, English Standard Version®), copyright © 2001 by Crossway, a publishing ministry of Good News Publishers. Used by permission. All rights reserved.

Scripture quotations marked (GNT) are from the Good News Translation in Today's English Version- Second Edition Copyright © 1992 by American Bible Society. Used by Permission.

Scripture marked (GW) is taken from GOD'S WORD®, © 1995 God's Word to the Nations. Used by permission of Baker Publishing Group.

CONTENTS

Introduction ix

The World and the Word 1
Lie Like Eden 9
Battle for Souls 13
Bloodshed and Forgiveness 21
The Barren Womb and the Life 29
Brother and Sister Keepers 33
The Coats and the Love 39
The Feet and the Authority 43
Face to Face and the Reveal 49
Finger of Judgment 53
The Eye and the Object of our Affection 60
The Kisses and the Intentions 65
The Pleasures and the Choices 68
The Follow and the End 72
Applying God's Love-truth and the Rebirth 75
Knowledge of Good and Evil 80
The Heart and God's Love-truth 87

INTRODUCTION

The word of God is the absolute love truth! There are many wonders in His word, but not all His wonders can be held in just one book! But for now, God has put what He wants us to know in that one book.

And many other signs truly did Jesus in the presence of his disciples, which are not written in this book: But these are written, that ye might believe that Jesus is the Christ, the Son of God; and that believing ye might have life through his name. John 20:30-31

And there are also many other things which Jesus did, the which, if they should be written every one, I suppose that even the world itself could not contain the books that should be written. Amen. John 21:25

Wow, that's a lot of books!

The Bible was inspired by the Lord most high!

All Scripture is inspired by God [breathed out by God; God-breathed]... 2 Timothy 3:16 EXB

Here are the very first words in the Bible. This is the first thing God wants us to know.

In the beginning God created the heaven and the earth. Genesis 1:1

And this is what God has to say about His thoughts and His ways. They are higher.

My thoughts are nothing like your thoughts, <u>says the Lord.</u> And my ways are far beyond anything you could imagine. For just as the heavens are higher than the earth, so my ways are higher than your ways and my thoughts higher than your thoughts. Isaiah 55:8-9 NLT

So, if God's ways and thoughts are higher than our ways and thoughts, as the heavens are higher than the earth higher, wouldn't we want to know what they are?

In the natural world, we are sure about some things. We are sure that hot is absolutely the opposite of cold, that light is absolutely the opposite of darkness, and that here on Earth, day is absolutely the opposite of night.

The Bible is filled with higher, absolute truths that we can be sure of. Salvation is one of those truths!

Maschil of Asaph.

For God is my King of old, working salvation in the midst of the earth. Psalm 74:12

Paul wrote,

For I am not ashamed of the gospel, because it is the power of God that brings salvation to everyone who believes: first to the Jew, then to the Gentile. Romans 1:16 NIV

Scriptures declaring salvation were not only written by Asaph and Paul, but by many others as well, at different times in history, all inspired by the same Holy Spirit of God, all coming together in divine harmony in one holy book, the Bible.

We are not separate from our words and our hearts, and neither is God. Just as our words and our hearts reveal who we are, Gods words and heart reveal who He is.

...for out of the abundance of the heart the mouth speaks. Matthew 12:34 NKJV

God is love.

Why wouldn't we want to read what is in God's heart? Even if you don't believe in a Creator God, what could it hurt to read the Book He is credited for writing? And even if you've picked the Bible up and read it a few times and thought it could not possibly be legit, please give this book a read. I have many wonderful things to share with you that you may not know! Yes, I am trying to convince you to read this book, because I have worked very hard to put the Scriptures together in a way that will help you see that the Bible a book filled with wonders written by a wonderful God. And if you are a believer and have read the Bible countless times, I think you will enjoy this book too.

And even though the Bible, inspired by God, was written by different men at different times in history it is consistent. In fact, we see things repeated throughout it that lead us to a message or messages.

We see fingers repeated in the Bible. When we follow fingers, we can find a message about judgment.

We've heard, *if we point a finger at someone else, we have three fingers pointing back at us.*

In the Old Testament, in the book of Exodus, Moses wrote that the Ten Commandments were written with the finger of God. The Ten Commandments are God's law. In the New Testament, John wrote that Jesus wrote on the ground with his finger when they were wanting to stone the adulterous woman.

We learn that God is the only One that can make good judgments because He is perfect.

We like to gain knowledge. We read book after book. We search the internet. We want to know stuff! Our brains can only know so much stuff! But God, He is all-knowing. He is omniscient. Omniscient is from two Latin words omnis, which means all, and scientia which means knowledge. So, God really does know all!

We learn math from math books, we learn history from history books, and we learn God from God's book. And the things we can learn there are way beyond just us, and we can only grasp these things by the help of the Holy Spirit.

We learn about the salvation of our souls in the Bible. It is the gospel of Jesus Christ.

Paul wrote.

You have been taught the holy Scriptures from childhood, and they have given you the wisdom to receive the salvation that comes by trusting in Christ Jesus. All Scripture is inspired by God and is useful to teach us what is true and to make us realize what is wrong in our lives. It corrects us when we are wrong and teaches us to do what is right. God uses it to prepare and equip his people to do every good work. 2 Timothy 3:15-17 NLT

God's word reveals Who He is.

God is love. 1 John 4:8

And His word is truth!

. . .thy word is truth. John 17:17

So, we could say God's word is God's absolute love-truth!

[God's] words all add up to the sum total: Truth. [His] righteous decisions are eternal. Psalm 119:160 The Message

The Holy Trinity, Father, Son and Holy Spirit are God's love-truth. The word of God tells about the Holy Trinity. We see Holy Trinity in the same vicinity when Jesus was baptized.

And **Jesus**, when he was baptized, went up straightway out of the water: and, lo, the heavens were opened unto him, and he saw the **Spirit of God** descending like a dove, and lighting upon him: And lo a **voice from heaven, saying, This is my beloved Son**, in whom I am well pleased. Matthew 3:16-17

World truths evolve because world truths are not perfect. God's love-truth remains constant because God's love-truth is perfect.

The Law of the Lord is perfect, giving new strength to the soul. The Law He has made known is sure, making the child-like wise. The Laws of the Lord are right, giving joy to the heart. The Word of the Lord is pure, giving light to the eyes. The fear of the Lord is pure, lasting forever. The Lord is always true and right in how He judges. The Word of the Lord is worth more than gold, even more than much fine gold. They are sweeter than honey, even honey straight from the comb. And by them Your servant is told to be careful. In obeying them there is great reward. Psalm 19:7-11NLV

God's love-truth reveals that good is very much different than evil.

And the world we live in, on a whole, is gray about good and evil in many ways. For instance, people know murder is evil, unless it is done in the name of, let's say, abortion. And most people know stealing is evil unless it is done in the name of, let's say, not tithing. But there is nothing gray about God's love-truth. God's love-truth is a rainbow, and all that a rainbow should be! A rainbow is anything but vague! It is up there! You can see it! It is bright and beautiful! It's a promise! The Holy Bible promises us that the God who created us, loves us! Anything contrary to that is a lie. And that's the God's absolute love-truth!

THE WORLD AND THE WORD

There are two kinds of people, people of the world, and people of God's Word. What they do does not make them of the world, or of the word of God, it is what they believe. The people of the world are mostly anti-Christ and anti-Christian, and of course, the people of the Word of God are pro Christ!

John wrote about two kinds of people.

"He who believes in Him is not condemned; but he who does not believe is condemned already, because he has not believed in the name of the only begotten Son of God. And this is the condemnation, that the light has come into the world, and men loved darkness rather than light, because their deeds were evil. For everyone practicing evil hates the light and does not come to the light, lest his deeds should be exposed. But he who does the truth comes to the light, that his deeds may be clearly seen, that they have been done in God." John 3:18-21 NKJV

Before we go any further, I want you to see who I am referring to throughout this book when I say, the devil, throughout the Bible he is called different things. The devil deceives the whole world.

And the great dragon was cast out, that old serpent, called the Devil, and Satan, which deceiveth the whole world: he was cast out into the earth, and his angels were cast out with him. Revelation 12:9

The devil is the god of this world and that is why the world, on a whole, is anti-Christ and anti-Christian. He darkens the minds of all that believe not, the light of the glorious gospel of Christ can't shine in an unbelieving heart.

And he did not many mighty works there because of their unbelief. Matthew 13:58

But if our gospel be hid, it is hid to them that are lost: In whom the god of this world hath blinded the minds of them which believe not, lest the light of the glorious gospel of Christ, who is the image of God, should shine unto them.. 2 Corinthians 4:3-4

The devil, the god of this world, rules in darkness by dangling the things that are in the world in front of people. The things that are in the world is summarized by three things: the lusts of the flesh, the lust of the eyes and the pride of life.

John wrote.

Love not the world, neither the things that are in the world. If any man love the world, the love of the Father is not in him. For all that is in the world, the lust of the flesh, and the lust of the eyes, and the pride of life, is not of the Father, but is of the world. 1 John 2:15-16

These things can hinder people from seeing the things of God. These things can even make people enemies of God and of God's children. The word of God is not welcome in a world filled with lust and pride, nor in a person that is filled with lust and pride because the light of God's word reproves such things.

John wrote.

...And this is the condemnation, that light is come into the world, and men loved darkness rather than light, because their deeds were evil. For every one that doeth evil hateth the light, neither cometh to the light, lest his deeds should be reproved. But he that doeth truth cometh to the light, that his deeds may be made manifest, that they are wrought in God. John 3:17-21

James wrote.

From whence come wars and fightings among you? come they not hence, even of your lusts that war in your members? Ye lust, and have not: ye kill, and desire to have, and cannot obtain: ye fight and war, yet ye have not, because ye ask not. Ye ask, and receive not, because ye ask amiss, that ye may consume it upon your lusts. Ye adulterers and adulteresses, know ye not that the friendship of the world is enmity with God? whosoever therefore will be a friend of the world is the enemy of God. Do ye think that the scripture saith in vain, The spirit that dwelleth in us lusteth to envy? But he giveth more grace. Wherefore he saith, God resisteth the proud, but giveth grace unto the humble. Submit yourselves therefore to God. Resist the devil, and he will flee from you. Draw nigh to God, and he will draw nigh to you. Cleanse your hands, ye sinners; and purify your hearts, ye double minded. James 4:1-8

Let us look through the Bible and see how the devil, *and I would think his angels that fell with him*, have used the things that are in the world to stop the word of God from growing in hearts. The word of God grows in hearts that believe it; that live it.

In Eden, that old serpent the devil deceived Eve by pulling her away from God's word into an unknown world of intrigue. He made her question what God really said about the tree of the knowledge of good and evil, and he had her look at the very tree. God had said if they were to eat of that tree, they would surely die. There are many things the devil can convince people to do by making them look at something with desire and keep them from thinking of the consequences.

And when the woman saw that the tree was good for food, and that it was pleasant to the eyes, and a tree to be desired to make one wise, she took of the fruit thereof, and did eat, and gave also unto her husband with her; and he did eat. Genesis 3:6

And Adam was not deceived, but the woman being deceived was in the transgression. 1 Timothy 2:14

When Adam and Eve ate of the tree their eyes were opened and they saw their flesh. Things were definitely different. They made aprons to cover, what would be from that day forth, their private parts. *There is significance in this, but not for this book.* They were afraid because they were naked. They ran and hid from God.

And the eyes of them both were opened, and they knew that they were naked; and they sewed fig leaves together, and made themselves aprons. And they heard the voice of the LORD God walking in the garden in the cool of the day: and Adam and his wife hid themselves from the presence of the LORD God amongst the trees of the garden.

And the LORD God called unto Adam, and said unto him, Where art thou? And he said, I heard thy voice in the garden, and I was afraid, because I was naked; and I hid myself. And he said, Who told thee that thou wast naked? Hast thou eaten of the tree, whereof I commanded thee that thou shouldest not eat? And the man said, The woman whom thou gavest to be with me, she gave me of the tree, and I did eat. And the LORD God said unto the woman, What is this that thou hast done? And the woman said, The serpent beguiled me, and I did eat. Genesis 3:7-13

The devil is the god of this world and he wants people to love the world and not God's word. He wants to keep people as far away from God's word as possible because God's word are the words of life.

Then said Jesus unto the twelve, Will ye also go away? Then Simon Peter answered him, Lord, to whom shall we go? thou hast the words of eternal life. John 6:67-68

The first two humans believed the devil's lie and *we all fell for it.*

Here is a love-truth that John wrote that we will see play out over and over as we look at hatred in this chapter.

Whosoever hateth his brother is a murderer: and ye know that no murderer hath eternal life abiding in him. 1 John 3:15

Hate runs rampant in this world and we see it a lot of the times between two sets of people, people of the world and people of God and that's what we will be looking at in this chapter.

First, we will look at the hate and division with the first two sons. It was the first account of sibling rivalry and it was bad. Cain despised the righteous ways of his brother. A righteous way is a sure sign someone is obeying God's word.

In this the children of God are manifest, and the children of the devil: whosoever doeth not righteousness is not of God, neither he that loveth not his brother. For this is the message that ye heard from the beginning, that we should love one another. Not as Cain, who was of that wicked one, and slew his brother. And wherefore slew he him? Because his own works were evil, and his brother's righteous. 1 John 3:10-12 Hate has no regard for human life.

Their offering to God revealed their heart for God.

And in process of time it came to pass, that Cain brought of the fruit of the ground an offering unto the LORD. And Abel, he also brought of the firstlings of his flock and of the fat thereof. And the LORD had respect unto Abel and to his offering: But unto Cain and to his offering he had not respect. And Cain was very wroth, and his countenance fell. Genesis 4:3-5

When one sibling does better than the other sibling there can be trouble, but murder? Abel's offering was from the first of his flock, and the fat thereof, and that sounds like a better offering than Cain's.

A ruler in Egypt came on the scene who did not know Joseph. He watched as God's children grew at an alarming rate right before his eyes. He was afraid they would become more and mightier than the Egyptians, and I'm sure, since he was king over Egypt, he knew these people worshipped another God, a God they served and a God they obeyed, not an Egyptian god. He resorted to murdering all their firstborn sons to slow the population. He was a proud king of Egypt, and Egypt was his main concern.

And the children of Israel were fruitful, and increased abundantly, and multiplied, and waxed exceeding mighty; and the land was filled with them. Now there arose up a new king over Egypt, which knew not Joseph. And he said unto his people, Behold, the people of the children of Israel are more and mightier than we: Come on, let us deal wisely with them; lest they multiply, and it come to pass, that, when there falleth out any war, they join also unto our enemies, and fight against us, and so get them up out of the land. . .And Pharaoh charged all his people, saying, Every son that is born ye shall cast into the river, and every daughter ye shall save alive. Exodus 1:7-10, 22 *Hate has no regard for human life.*

Haman was a prince in the kingdom of King Ahasuerus. All the king's servants bowed to him, but Mordecai, a Jew, did not bow to him. This made Haman very angry. Haman conspired to have all the Jews destroyed. He pointed out to the king that these people were different from other people and were not keeping the king's laws.

And Haman said unto king Ahasuerus, There is a certain people scattered abroad and dispersed among the people in all the provinces of thy kingdom; and their laws are diverse from all people; neither keep they the king's laws: therefore it is not for the king's profit to suffer them. If it please the king, let it be written that they may be destroyed: and I will pay ten thousand talents of silver to the hands of those that have the charge of the business, to bring it into the king's treasuries. And the king took his ring from his hand, and gave it unto Haman the son of Hammedatha the Agagite, the Jews' enemy. Esther 3:8-10 *Hate has no regard for human life.*

When Jesus was born, King Herod heard that a King of the Jews had been born. King Herod knew the Jews were known as the children of God. He asked the wise men to show him to the child so he could go worship him, but the wise men were wise, and they knew better. They eluded him. Herod was proud and it made him angry that they mocked him by doing that. *An angel told Joseph that Herod would try to destroy Jesus and told them to go to Egypt. (Matthew 2:16)* And Herod had all the children in Bethlehem from two years old and under killed. Hate has not regard for human life.

Now when Jesus was born in Bethlehem of Judaea in the days of Herod the king, behold, there came wise men from the east to Jerusalem, Saying, Where is he that is born King of the Jews? for we have seen his star in the east, and are come to worship him. When Herod the king had heard these things, he was troubled, and all Jerusalem with him. Matthew 2:1-3

Then Herod, when he had privily called the wise men, enquired of them diligently what time the star appeared. And he sent them to Bethlehem, and said, Go and search diligently for the young child; and when ye have found him, bring me word again, that I may come and worship him also. Matthew 2:7-8

Then Herod, when he saw that he was mocked of the wise men, was exceeding wroth, and sent forth, and slew all the children that were in Bethlehem, and in all the coasts thereof, from two years old and under, according to the time which he had diligently inquired of the wise men. Matthew 2:16 *Hate has no regard for human life.*

When Jesus was before Pilate, the crowd had a choice because Pilate had offered to release a prisoner to them. They were to choose between Jesus, the King of the Jews, or Barabbas, a murderer. The chief priests and elders persuaded the people to choose the murderer. *And it was the words and deeds of Jesus up to that point that had caused the division and the religious leaders to hate him so; they were jealous of Him.*

Now at that feast the governor was wont to release unto the people a prisoner, whom they would. And they had then a notable prisoner, called Barabbas. Therefore when they were gathered together, Pilate said unto them, Whom will ye that I release unto you? Barabbas, or Jesus which is called Christ? For he knew that for envy they had delivered him. When he was set down on the judgment seat, his wife sent unto him, saying, Have thou nothing to do with that just man: for I have suffered many things this day in a dream because of him. But the chief priests and elders persuaded the multitude that they should ask Barabbas, and destroy Jesus. Matthew 27;15-20 *Hate has no regard for human life.*

And the schemers were still scheming even after Jesus died. They remembered what Jesus said about rising again the third day. They could never let people believe that for their power was at stake. They conspired together and came up with a lie, a lie that is still told today. And it is a lie that helps to darken the minds of those that do not believe the gospel of Jesus Christ.

Now the next day, that followed the day of the preparation, the chief priests and Pharisees came together unto Pilate, Saying, Sir, we remember that that deceiver said, while he was yet alive, After three days I will rise again. Command therefore that the sepulchre be made sure until the third day, lest his disciples come by night, and steal him away, and say unto the people, He is risen from the dead: so the last error shall be worse than the first. Pilate said unto them, Ye have a watch: go your way, make it as sure as ye can. So they went, and made the sepulchre sure, sealing the stone, and setting a watch. Matthew 27:62-66

The Father sent the Holy Spirit to empower His disciples to preach the gospel of Jesus Christ. And when they preached, people responded to it in two different ways, as it still is today.

And when they heard of the resurrection of the dead, some mocked: and others said, We will hear thee again of this matter. Acts 17:32

Before we believe God's love-truth, the gospel of Jesus Christ, we were of the world and we were enemies of God in our minds. The lust of the flesh, the lust of the eyes, or the pride of life, or a combination of all three shaped our thinking. We thought like the world, we acted like the world, we loved the world and the things in the world. When we accept Jesus, we love the things of God. We love God's love-truth.

People that live by faith in God's love-truth are hated by the world because the God's love-truth goes against the things that are in this world.

By faith these people overthrew kingdoms, ruled with justice, and received what God had promised them. They shut the mouths of lions, quenched the flames of fire, and escaped death by the edge of the sword. Their weakness was turned to strength. They became strong in battle and put whole armies to flight. Women received their loved ones back again from death. But others were tortured, refusing to turn from God in order to be set free. They placed their hope in a better life after the resurrection. Some were jeered at, and their backs were cut open with whips. Others were chained in prisons. Some died by stoning, some were sawed in half, and others were killed with the sword. Some went about wearing skins of sheep and goats, destitute and oppressed and mistreated. *They were too good for this world,* wandering over deserts and mountains, hiding in caves and holes in the ground. All these people earned a good reputation because of their faith, yet none of them received all that God had promised. For God had something better in mind for us, so that they would not reach perfection without us. Hebrews 11:33-40 NLT

JESUS CHRIST LIGHT

Who gave himself for our sins, that he might deliver us from this present evil world, according to the will of God and our Father: Galatians 1:4

LIE LIKE EDEN

The devil is a liar.
   For you are the children of your father the devil, and you love to do the evil things he does. He was a murderer from the beginning. He has always hated the truth, because there is no truth in him. When he lies, it is consistent with his character; for he is a liar and the father of lies. John 8:44 NLT

And the devil still lies as he did in Eden. He will often start out with something that looks good and put bad at the end, where it is hardly noticed. The first lie went a little something like this.

And the serpent said unto the woman,
You shall not surely die
Your eyes shall be opened
You shall be as gods
Knowing good
and
evil. Genesis 3:4-5

The devil is subtil when he lies against God's love- truth and he teaches people to lie the same way. He is a lying snake and wants to keep as many people as he can in the dark about life, this life and the life hereafter. He doesn't want people to think about what happens after they die. He doesn't want them to think about heaven and hell. He doesn't want them to think about good and evil.

Although I don't think the serpent was crawling around on his belly when he tempted Eve, I want us to think about how low a natural snake is. To do that, think about the sun, the moon, the stars, the clouds, mankind, cattle, birds, then think about, a snake. You can't get any lower than a snake.

As we go through the Bible, we will see how people have a way of lying against God's love-truth and make it sound right. They are subtil, and the lies go sometimes undetected.

The chief priests, the scribes, and the elders of the people consulted together how that they might take Jesus by subtilty and kill him.

They found two false witnesses that said.

This fellow said, I am able to destroy the temple of God, and to build it in three days.

After that, they asked Jesus plainly.

Tell us whether You are the Christ, the Son of God.

Jesus answered them with a visual.

Hereafter shall ye see the Son of man sitting on the right hand of power and coming in the clouds of heaven.

And that's when they cried, blasphemy and found him guilty of death!

Now the chief priests, and elders, and all the council, sought false witness against Jesus, to put him to death; But found none: yea, though many false witnesses came, yet found they none. At the last came two false witnesses, And said, This fellow said, I am able to destroy the temple of God, and to build it in three days. And the high priest arose, and said unto him, Answerest thou nothing? what is it which these witness against thee? But Jesus held his peace. And the high priest answered and said unto him, I adjure thee by the living God, that thou tell us whether thou be the Christ, the Son of God. Jesus saith unto him, Thou hast said: nevertheless I say unto you, Hereafter shall ye see the Son of man sitting on the right hand of power, and coming in the clouds of heaven. Then the high priest rent his clothes, saying, He hath spoken blasphemy; what further need have we of witnesses? behold, now ye have heard his blasphemy. What think ye? They answered and said, He is guilty of death. Matthew 26:59-66

The lies of the sorcerer, Elymas were subtil as he withstood the God's love-truth. Paul exposed him for what he really was, he told him he was full of all subtilty and all mischief, a child of the devil, an enemy of all righteousness, perverting the right ways of the Lord.

And when they had gone through the isle unto Paphos, they found a certain sorcerer, a false prophet, a Jew, whose name was Bar-jesus: Which was with the deputy of the country, Sergius Paulus, a prudent man; who called for Barnabas and Saul, and desired to hear the word of God. But Elymas the sorcerer (for so is his name by interpretation) withstood them, seeking to turn away the deputy from the faith. Then Saul, (who also is called Paul,) filled with the Holy Ghost, set his eyes on him, And said, O full of all subtilty and all mischief, thou child of the devil, thou enemy of all righteousness, wilt thou not cease to pervert the right ways of the Lord? Acts 13:6-10

The lies of false leaders and teachers in the church are also subtil. Paul warned the Corinthians how deceivers deceive with the same subtilty the serpent deceived Eve with. What the devil told Eve seemed right, but it so very wrong. Paul told the Corinthians not to receive another Jesus, and not to receive another gospel other than the one they had preached to them. So, whatever these false one's were saying, it sounded right.

But I fear, lest by any means, as the serpent beguiled Eve through his subtilty, so your minds should be corrupted from the simplicity that is in Christ. For if he that cometh preacheth another Jesus, whom we have not preached, or if ye receive another spirit, which ye have not received, or another gospel, which ye have not accepted. . .For such are false apostles, deceitful workers, transforming themselves into the apostles of Christ. And no marvel; for Satan himself is transformed into an angel of light. Therefore it is no great thing if his ministers also be transformed as the ministers of righteousness; whose end shall be according to their works. 2 Corinthians 11:3-4; 13-15

God's love-truth is our weapon against the hate generated lies about God's love that are out there. It will keep us grounded in His love.

Then we will no longer be immature like children. We won't be tossed and blown about by every wind of new teaching. We will not be influenced when people try to trick us with lies so clever they sound like the truth. Instead, we will speak the truth in love, growing in every way more and more like Christ, who is the head of his body, the church. Ephesians 4:14-15 NLT

JESUS CHRIST LIGHT

Be sure you are not led away by the teaching of those who have nothing worth saying and only plan to deceive you. That teaching is not from Christ. It is only human tradition and comes from the powers that influence this world. Colossians 2:8 ERV

BATTLE FOR SOULS

Every superhero movie we have ever seen is a battle between good and evil. The heroes are good, the villains are evil. The heroes want the people free. The villains want to control the people.

The hero is God.

God is love. 1 John 4:8

The hero is out to save.

For God so loved the world, that he gave his only begotten Son, that whosoever believeth in him should not perish, but have everlasting life. John 3:16

God's superpower is love. The only power the devil has to try to strip God of His power is deception. He can never take God's power from Him, but he is scheming all the time how to take God's love away from the people in the world.

So, as we follow the battles in the Bible, we see that the battles are for souls.

We know who wins this epic battle between good and evil from the beginning.

Because thou hast done this, thou art cursed above all cattle, and above every beast of the field; upon thy belly shalt thou go, and dust shalt thou eat all the days of thy life: And I will put enmity between thee and the woman, and between thy seed and her seed; it shall bruise thy head, and thou shalt bruise his heel. Genesis 3: 14-15

But the enemy wants to keep who the victor is, in the dark.

When the Lord God cursed the serpent in the beginning, He was saying how He would give all souls an opportunity to come back to Him, even the souls born before Christ.

Before Christ, people looked ahead to Jesus, the One the prophets foretold of.

During Christ, people could see Jesus with their very own eyes.

After Christ rose again, people look to the witness accounts that looked upon Him and walked with Him. These accounts are recorded in God's Word.

The Bible is filled with Jesus from Genesis to Revelation.

Even the ones who got to see Jesus with their own eyes had to have faith in Him. They had to believe He is who He says He is, the Son of God.

Jesus Christ would be the seed of the woman and would be the victor that would crush the serpent's head. And Jesus Christ would have to leave heaven in order to do so. Jesus is God's superpower love in the flesh, and He came all the way from heaven to earth to fight for souls!

For Christ also hath once suffered for sins, the just for the unjust, that he might bring us to God, being put to death in the flesh, but quickened by the Spirit: 1 Peter 3:18

While Moses was up on the mountain hearing from God, there was a battle for souls taking place in the camp below. Moses was up on the mountain a long time and the people got restless. They didn't think he was going to come back down so they asked Aaron to make them a golden god to lead them. When Moses came down and saw their shameful behavior, *Aaron referred to it as mischief, or another word would be evil,* Moses told them if they were on the Lord's side they could come to his side.

And Moses said unto Aaron, What did this people unto thee, that thou hast brought so great a sin upon them? And Aaron said, Let not the anger of my lord wax hot: thou knowest the people, that they are set on mischief. For they said unto me, Make us gods, which shall go before us: for as for this Moses, the man that brought us up out of the land of Egypt, we wot not what is become of him. And I said unto them, Whosoever hath any gold, let them break it off. So they gave it me: then I cast it into the fire, and there came out this calf. And when Moses saw that the people were naked; (for Aaron had made them naked unto their shame among their enemies:) Then Moses stood in the gate of the camp, and said, Who is on the LORD's side? let him come unto me. And all the sons of Levi gathered themselves together unto him. Exodus 32:21-26

When we read all of Exodus 32, we know what became of those that did not choose the Lord's side.

When Jesus was led of the Spirit into the wilderness to be tempted of the devil, He fought with words. Each temptation thrown at Him was a lie against a love-truth about His Father, and Jesus fought each lie with, *it is written*!

It was a fight of faith for us more than for Himself. We overcome temptation the very same way.

The first temptation was a lie about Jehovah-Jireh, the Lord Provider. (Abraham and the sacrifice. Genesis 22:1-14)

The tempter tried to get Jesus to rely on Himself and not on His Father...

When the tempter tempted the Bread of heaven, saying, "If thou be the Son of God, command that these stones be made bread." Jesus answered, **"It is written, Man shall not live by bread alone, but by every word that proceedeth out of the mouth of God."** Matthew 4:3-4

The second temptation was a lie about Shalom, the Lord is peace. (Gideon and the sign. Judges 6:13-24)

The devil took him up into the holy city, and setteth him on a pinnacle of the temple, and said to the One Who does give angels their charge, "If thou be the Son of God, cast thyself down: for it is written, He shall give his angels charge concerning thee: and in their hands they shall bear thee up, lest at any time thou dash thy foot against a stone." Jesus said unto him, **"It is written again, Thou shalt not tempt the Lord thy God."** Matthew 4:5-7

The third temptation was a lie about Adonai, God as Master. (Abraham and the promise. Genesis 15:1-6)

The devil took him up into an exceeding high mountain, and showed the King of Kings all the kingdoms of the world, and the glory of them; and said unto him, "All these things will I give thee, if thou wilt fall down and worship me." Jesus unto him, "Get thee hence, Satan: **for**

it is written, Thou shalt worship the Lord thy God, and him only shalt thou serve." Matthew 4:8-10

The battle is for souls, and Jesus compared soul winning with fishing. Just as the disciples caught boat loads of fish at Jesus' word, we catch souls the same way. We win souls with the God's love-truth, the gospel of Jesus Christ.

Once, Jesus told his disciples to launch out into the deep and let down their nets and when they obeyed Him, they ended up with a big catch. Simon was skeptical of catching anything for they had been fishing all night long, but he obeyed what Jesus said, and he was astonished at the outcome.

Jesus said unto Simon, Launch out into the deep, and let down your nets for a draught. And Simon answering said unto him, Master, we have toiled all the night, and have taken nothing: nevertheless at thy word I will let down the net. And when they had this done, they inclosed a great multitude of fishes: and their net brake. And they beckoned unto their partners, which were in the other ship, that they should come and help them. And they came, and filled both the ships, so that they began to sink. When Simon Peter saw it, he fell down at Jesus' knees, saying, Depart from me; for I am a sinful man, O Lord. For he was astonished, and all that were with him, at the draught of the fishes which they had taken: And so was also James, and John, the sons of Zebedee, which were partners with Simon. And Jesus said unto Simon, Fear not; from henceforth thou shalt catch men. Luke 5:4-10

The fruit of those who are right with God is a tree of life, and he who wins souls is wise. Proverbs 11:30 NLV

Even after Jesus rose again from the dead, He told His disciples how to fish and He also gave them fish to eat. The Father draws the souls to Himself, we let down the net of God's love-truth about Jesus whenever and wherever the opportunity arises to share.

And he said unto them, Cast the net on the right side of the ship, and ye shall find. They cast therefore, and now they were not able to draw it for the multitude of fishes. Therefore that disciple whom Jesus loved saith unto Peter, It is the Lord. Now when Simon Peter heard that it was the Lord, he girt his fisher's coat unto him, (for he was naked,) and did cast himself into the sea. And the other disciples came in a little ship; (for they were not far from land, but as it were two hundred cubits,) dragging the net with fishes. As soon then as they were come to land, they saw a fire of coals there, and fish laid thereon, and bread. Jesus saith unto them, Bring of the fish which ye have now caught. Simon Peter went up, and drew the net to land full of great fishes, an hundred and fifty and three: and for all there were so many, yet was not the net broken. Jesus saith unto them, Come and dine. And none of the disciples durst ask him, Who art thou? knowing that it was the Lord. Jesus then cometh, and taketh bread, and giveth them, and fish likewise. This is now the third time that Jesus shewed himself to his disciples, after that he was risen from the dead. . .John 21:6-14

Let's look at a famous fish story, the story of Jonah and the big fish. God told Jonah to go fishing for souls by preaching in Ninevah. This was Jonah's opportunity to fight for souls by giving them a warning from God, but Jonah rose up to flee.

Now the word of the LORD came unto Jonah the son of Amittai, saying, Arise, go to Nineveh, that great city, and cry against it; for their wickedness is come up before me.

But Jonah rose up to flee unto Tarshish from the presence of the LORD, and went down to Joppa; and he found a ship going to Tarshish: so he paid the fare thereof, and went down into it, to go with them unto Tarshish *from the presence of the LORD.* Jonah 1:1-3

But the LORD sent out a great wind into the sea, and there was a mighty tempest in the sea, so that the ship was like to be broken. 1:4

After crying out to their gods and throwing stuff overboard, the mariners finally came to Jonah, who was sleeping. 1:5

Their so called gods were not listening, so perhaps Jonah's God would.

. . .What meanest thou, O sleeper? arise, call upon thy God, if so be that *God will think upon us, that we perish not.* Jonah 1:6

Jonah told them if they threw him overboard they would be saved. They didn't want to do it, but they did.

So they took up Jonah, and cast him forth into the sea: and the sea ceased from her raging. Then the men feared the LORD exceedingly, and offered a sacrifice unto the LORD, and made vows. 1:15-16

They found out Jonah's God was bigger than their gods.

Jonah's God sent out the great wind on the sea, and prepared a great fish in the sea to swallow up Jonah.

Now the LORD had prepared a great fish to swallow up Jonah. And Jonah was in the belly of the fish three days and three nights. Jonah 1:17

After spending three days and three nights in the belly of the fish, Jonah repented and went and preached to the city.

So Jonah arose, and went unto Nineveh, according to the word of the LORD. Now Nineveh was an exceeding great city of three days' journey. And Jonah began to enter into the city a day's journey, and he cried, and said, Yet forty days, and Nineveh shall be overthrown. So the people of Nineveh believed God, and proclaimed a fast, and put on sackcloth, from the greatest of them even to the least of them. Jonah 3:3-5

After Jonah preached, the people repented and that's where we find out why he didn't want to go preach to them in the first place. It was a very selfish reason. It was his pride that made him run away from the call of God. Pride is a weapon of the enemy to stop the truth from getting out.

But it displeased Jonah exceedingly, and he was very angry. And he prayed unto the LORD, and said, I pray thee, O LORD, was not this my saying, when I was yet in my country? Therefore I fled before unto Tarshish: for I knew that thou art a gracious God, and merciful, slow to anger, and of great kindness, and repentest thee of the evil. Jonah 4:1-3

I think it ironic that *Jonah ran from God, refusing to fish for souls and God had a big fish catch Jonah.*

We want to fight for souls because Jesus said the end of the world will be like a net cast into the sea to gather every kind and what ends up in the net will be sorted. The just will be gathered into vessels, and the wicked will be cast away.

Again, the kingdom of heaven is like unto a net, that was cast into the sea, and gathered of every kind: Which, when it was full, they drew to shore, and sat down, and gathered the good into vessels, but cast the bad away. So shall it be at the end of the world: the angels shall come forth, and sever the wicked from among the just, Matthew 13:47-49

There is a harvest for souls that we need to be engaged in. We should pray for workers and we should be workers in the harvest. The harvest for souls is where our battlefield is.

But when he saw the multitudes, he was moved with compassion on them, because they fainted, and were scattered abroad, as sheep having no shepherd. Then saith he unto his disciples, The harvest truly is plenteous, but the labourers are few; Pray ye therefore the Lord of the harvest, that he will send forth labourers into his harvest. Matthew 9:36-38

And the battle for souls will continue until time is no more, so we should remain strong in battle, by staying equipped.

Please read the following Scriptures in their entirety for clearer understanding.

<u>We can</u>

Be strong in the Lord and in the power of His might

Put on the armor of God and stand against the wiles of the devil

Pray always with all prayer and supplication in the Spirit

Watch in prayer with all perseverance and supplication for all saints Ephesians 6:10-18

Walk in the Spirit

Be led of the Spirit

Have the fruits of the Spirit; love, joy, peace, longsuffering, gentleness, goodness, faith, meekness, temperance. Galatians 5:16-23

Study the word of truth

Ask God for the wisdom from above James 1:5, 3:17-18

Bring into captivity every thought to the obedience of Christ 2 Corinthians 10:3-5

Follow after righteousness, godliness, faith, love patience, meekness 1 Timothy 6:9-12

Seek God's kingdom first Matthew 6:25:34

Believe the love of God and dwell in it 1 John 4:16

We want to tell souls about Jesus Christ so their names will be found in the Lamb's Book of Life and awake to everlasting life and not everlasting contempt.

And at that time shall Michael stand up, the great prince which standeth for the children of thy people: and there shall be a time of trouble, such as never was since there was a nation even to that same time: and at that time thy people shall be delivered, every one that shall be found written in the book. And many of them that sleep in the dust of the earth shall awake, some to everlasting life, and some to shame and everlasting contempt. And they that be wise shall shine as the brightness of the firmament; and they that turn many to righteousness as the stars for ever and ever. Daniel12:1-3

JESUS CHRIST LIGHT

Having made known unto us the mystery of his will, according to his good pleasure which he hath purposed in himself: That in the dispensation of the fulness of times he might gather together in one all things in Christ, both which are in heaven, and which are on earth; even in him: Ephesians 1:9-10

BLOODSHED AND FORGIVENESS

When we follow bloodshed through the Bible, the message we can see is the message of forgiveness. Forgiveness is a grace that sets free, holding on to offenses is a prison.

Before we get too deep in Scripture, I want to make a point here, so we can get a better grasp why blood is necessary for our salvation and forgiveness.

We give blood to one another to save one another, why can't God give His blood to save the whole wide world?

The blood used as a sin offering for forgiveness in the Old Testament or law of Moses was the blood of animals. The blood used as a sin offering for forgiveness in the New Testament or the grace of God is the blood of Jesus Christ.

The old system under the law of Moses was only a shadow, a dim preview of the good things to come, not the good things themselves. The sacrifices under that system were repeated again and again, year after year, but they were never able to provide perfect cleansing for those who came to worship. If they could have provided perfect cleansing, the sacrifices would have stopped, for the worshipers would have been purified once for all time, and their feelings of guilt would have disappeared. But instead, those sacrifices actually reminded them of their sins year after year. For it is not possible for the blood of bulls and goats to take away sins. That is why, when Christ came into the world, he said to God, "You did not want animal sacrifices or sin offerings. But you have given me a body to offer. You were not pleased with burnt offerings or other offerings for sin. Then I said, 'Look, I have come to do your will, O God—as is written about me in the Scriptures.' First, Christ said, "You did not want animal sacrifices or sin offerings or burnt offerings or other offerings for sin, nor were you pleased with them" (though they are required by the law of Moses). Then he said, "Look, I have come to do your will." He cancels the first covenant in order to put the second into effect. For God's will was for us to be made holy by the sacrifice of the body of Jesus Christ, once for all time. Hebrews 10:1-10 NLT

When Cain shed his brother's blood, the voice of his brother's blood cried out to God from the earth! What was it crying out? Perhaps it was letting God know what was done to him in secret so there would be justice. Good deeds are done for all to see; evil deeds are done in the dark. And God knows about them all.

Cain became a fugitive in the earth, because his sin would now hide him from the face of God. The first prayer in the Bible was actually prayed by Cain. He asked God to save him from people who would try to kill him. God did this by promising retribution seven-fold to anyone that would kill Cain and God set a mark on Cain so others would not kill him. Cain's sin was murder and now he was afraid of being murdered. God marked him so he wouldn't have to be afraid of being murdered.

And Cain talked with Abel his brother: and it came to pass, when they were in the field, that Cain rose up against Abel his brother, and slew him. And the Lord said unto Cain, Where is Abel thy brother? And he said, I know not: Am I my brother's keeper? And he said, What hast thou done? the voice of thy brother's blood crieth unto me from the ground. And now art thou cursed from the earth, which hath opened her mouth to receive thy brother's blood from thy hand; When thou tillest the ground, it shall not henceforth yield unto thee her strength; a fugitive and a vagabond shalt thou be in the earth. And Cain said unto the Lord, My punishment is greater than I can bear. Behold, thou hast driven me out this day from the face of the earth; and from thy face shall I be hid; and I shall be a fugitive and a vagabond in the earth; and it shall come to pass, that every one that findeth me shall slay me. And the Lord said unto him, Therefore whosoever slayeth Cain, vengeance shall be taken on him sevenfold. And the Lord set a mark upon Cain, lest any finding him should kill him. Genesis 4:8-15

Abel is mentioned in Hebrews, chapter eleven.

Because Abel had faith, he gave a better gift in worship to God than Cain. His gift pleased God. Abel was right with God. Abel died, but by faith he is still speaking to us. Hebrews 11:4 NLV

Lamech shed blood too but it wasn't murder, it was self-defense. He knew the punishment for anyone who killed Cain, was seven times and that if anyone killed him, they should be punished seventy-seven times.

One day Lamech said to his wives, "Adah and Zillah, hear my voice; listen to me, you wives of Lamech. I have killed a man who attacked me, a young man who wounded me. If someone who kills Cain is punished seven times, then the one who kills me will be punished seventy-seven times!" Genesis 4:23-24 NLT

This reminds me of what Jesus told Peter about forgiveness. We should be as forgiving to others as God is to us, always ready!

For thou, Lord, art good, and ready to forgive; and plenteous in mercy unto all them that call upon thee. Psalm 86:5

Then came Peter to him, and said, Lord, how oft shall my brother sin against me, and I forgive him? till seven times? Jesus saith unto him, I say not unto thee, Until seven times: but, Until seventy times seven. Matthew 18:21-22

The earth was filled with violence before the great flood and more than likely there was a lot of blood shed happening.

The earth also was corrupt before God, and the earth was filled with violence. Genesis 6:11

When Noah and his family emerged from the ark, God laid down the law about bloodshed. When Cain shed blood, there was no death penalty. After the flood there was a death penalty for bloodshed.

. . .And surely your blood of your lives will I require; at the hand of every beast will I require it, and at the hand of man; at the hand of every man's brother will I require the life of man. Whoso sheddeth man's blood, by man shall his blood be shed: for in the image of God made he man. Genesis 9:1-6

The brothers of Joseph didn't shed their brother's blood, but they wanted to. Reuben talked them out of it. He told them not to shed their brother's blood but just throw him in the pit. He was planning to come back and rescue Joseph later. But while they were eating, some Ishmeelites on their way to Egypt, passed by and they sold their brother to them for twenty pieces of silver. Reuben was not a part of this scheme for he was away at the time. They shed the blood of a goat and dipped Joseph's coat in the blood to show to their father, and their father mourned for his son.

Later when Joseph's brothers had to go to Egypt to get corn in the time of famine, they came face to face with their brother again, though they didn't recognize it was him. When Joseph told them they had to bring their youngest brother back with them to prove they were not spies, Rueben was sure this was blood for blood payback for what they had done to Joseph. He was basically telling his brothers, I told you so. Taken from Genesis 37:20-34; 42:20-22

Later in life, Joseph forgives his brothers.

And when Joseph's brethren saw that their father was dead, they said, Joseph will peradventure hate us, and will certainly requite us all the evil which we did unto him. And they sent a messenger unto Joseph, saying, Thy father did command before he died, saying, So shall ye say unto Joseph, Forgive, I pray thee now, the trespass of thy brethren, and their sin; for they did unto thee evil: and now, we pray thee, forgive the trespass of the servants of the God of thy father. And Joseph wept when they spake unto him. And his brethren also went and fell down before his face; and they said, Behold, we be thy servants. And Joseph said unto them, Fear not: for am I in the place of God? But as for you, ye thought evil against me; but God meant it unto good, to bring to pass, as it is this day, to save much people alive. Now therefore fear ye not: I will nourish you, and your little ones. And he comforted them, and spake kindly unto them. Genesis 50:15-21

The last plague in Egypt was the death of the firstborn of Egypt. *The plague of sin leads to death.* Moses instructed the elders of Israel to kill a lamb per household and put the blood on the doors posts so death would not come into their houses.

Then Moses called for all the elders of Israel, and said unto them, Draw out and take you a lamb according to your families, and kill the Passover. And ye shall take a bunch of hyssop, and dip it in the blood that is in the bason, and strike the lintel and the two side posts with the blood that is in the bason; and none of you shall go out at the door of his house until the morning. For the LORD will pass through to smite the Egyptians; and when he seeth the blood upon the lintel, and on the two side posts, the LORD will pass over the door, and will not suffer the destroyer to come in unto your houses to smite you. Exodus 12:21-23

When the blood of Jesus Christ is applied to our hearts, death cannot come.

Jesus said unto her, I am the resurrection, and the life: he that believeth in me, though he were dead, yet shall he live: And whosoever liveth and believeth in me shall never die. . .John 11:25-26

Judas betrayed the innocent blood of Jesus Christ, the only blood that can wash away the sins of the guilty; the only blood that can provide complete forgiveness.

And ye know that he was manifested to take away our sins; and in him is no sin. 1 John 3:5

The chief priests took the silver pieces they had given Judas to betray Jesus and bought a field to bury strangers in. They called the field, The Field of Blood.

Then Judas, which had betrayed him, when he saw that he was condemned, repented himself, and brought again the thirty pieces of silver to the chief priests and elders, Saying, I have sinned in that I have betrayed the innocent blood. And they said, What is that to us? see thou to that. And he cast down the pieces of silver in the temple, and departed, and went and hanged himself. And the chief priests took the silver pieces, and said, It is not lawful for to put them into the treasury, because it is the price of blood. And they took counsel, and bought with them the potter's field, to bury strangers in. Wherefore that field was called, The field of blood, unto this day. Then was fulfilled that which was spoken by Jeremy the prophet, saying, And they took the thirty pieces of silver, the price of him that was valued, whom they of the children of Israel did value; And gave them for the potter's field, as the Lord appointed me. Matthew 27:3-10

Pilate did not want the shed blood of Jesus Christ on his hands and he even washed his hands to show he would have no part of it, but the people cried out, "His blood be on us, and on our children."

Pilate saith unto them, What shall I do then with Jesus which is called Christ? They all say unto him, Let him be crucified. And the governor said, Why, what evil hath he done? But they cried out the more, saying, Let him be crucified. When Pilate saw that he could prevail nothing, but that rather a tumult was made, he took water, and washed his hands before the multitude, saying, I am innocent of the blood of this just person: see ye to it. Then answered all the people, and said, His blood be on us, and on our children. Then released he Barabbas unto them: and when he had scourged Jesus, he delivered him to be crucified. Matthew 27:22-26

Stephen was a martyr. His blood was shed because resisters of the truth couldn't handle the truth. Stephen was a follower of Christ and he forgave them for shedding his blood before God received his spirit.

"You stubborn people! You are heathen at heart and deaf to the truth. Must you forever resist the Holy Spirit? That's what your ancestors did, and so do you! Name one prophet your ancestors didn't persecute! They even killed the ones who predicted the coming of the Righteous One—the Messiah whom you betrayed and murdered. You deliberately disobeyed God's law, even though you received it from the hands of angels." The Jewish leaders were infuriated by Stephen's accusation, and they shook their fists at him in rage. But Stephen, full of the Holy Spirit, gazed steadily into heaven and saw the glory of God, and he saw Jesus standing in the place of honor at God's right hand. And he told them, "Look, I see the heavens opened and the Son of Man standing in the place of honor at God's right hand!" Then they put their hands over their ears and began shouting. They rushed at him and dragged him out of the city and began to stone him. His accusers took off their coats and laid them at the feet of a young man named Saul. As they stoned him, Stephen prayed, "Lord Jesus, receive my spirit." He fell to his knees, shouting, "Lord, don't charge them with this sin!" And with that, he died. Acts 7:51-60 NLT

People were going to John the Baptist to be water baptized. When

Jesus came to be baptized, he called Him the Lamb of God. The people would immediately associate lamb of God with the forgiveness of their sins.

The next day John seeth Jesus coming unto him, and saith, Behold the Lamb of God, which taketh away the sin of the world. John 1:29

The Blood of Jesus speaks better things than that of Abel. The blood of Jesus speaks forgiveness.

But ye are come unto mount Sion, and unto the city of the living God, the heavenly Jerusalem, and to an innumerable company of angels, To the general assembly and church of the firstborn, which are written in heaven, and to God the Judge of all, and to the spirits of just men made perfect, And to Jesus the mediator of the new covenant, and to the blood of sprinkling, that speaketh better things than that of Abel. Hebrews 12:22-24

The blood of Jesus was shed in the garden in His tears.

And being in an agony he prayed more earnestly: and his sweat was as it were great drops of blood falling down to the ground. Luke 22:44

The blood of Jesus was shed when they pierced His side.

But one of the soldiers with a spear pierced his side, and forthwith came there out blood and water. John 19:34

On the cross, one thief saw a Savior, the other did not. One was forgiven that day, the other, probably not.

And one of the malefactors which were hanged railed on him, saying, If thou be Christ, save thyself and us. But the other answering rebuked him, saying, Dost not thou fear God, seeing thou art in the same condemnation? And we indeed justly; for we receive the due reward of our deeds: but this man hath done nothing amiss. And he said unto Jesus, Lord, remember me when thou comest into thy kingdom. And Jesus said unto him, Verily I say unto thee, To day shalt thou be with me in paradise. Luke 23:39-43

And before Jesus gave up His Spirit to His Father, He cried out for them all, forgiveness.

Father, forgive them; for they know not what they do. Luke 23:34

When we think of bloodshed, we think of murder. But the blood that was shed on the cross was not murder, it was given, given to give life! The blood of Jesus Christ is precious because it paid a precious price. It bought souls.

Forasmuch as ye know that ye were not redeemed with corruptible things, as silver and gold, from your vain conversation received by tradition from your fathers; But with the precious blood of Christ, as of a lamb without blemish and without spot: 1 Peter 1:18-19

When someone has a disease in their blood, they can sometimes get a blood transfusion to fix it. We are born into this world with the disease of sin in our blood. We will not be at ease until we are healed of that disease. No matter what we do, we will not get better, but we will only grow worse until we reach out to Jesus. Jesus gave His blood for us.

JESUS CHRIST LIGHT

That is why the Tabernacle and everything in it, which were copies of things in heaven, had to be purified by the blood of animals. But the real things in heaven had to be purified with far better sacrifices than the blood of animals. For Christ did not enter into a holy place made with human hands, which was only a copy of the true one in heaven. He entered into heaven itself to appear now before God on our behalf. Hebrews 9:23-24 NLT

THE BARREN WOMB AND THE LIFE

A barren womb can be considered a dead womb. Many times, in Scripture we see a barren womb, but eventually God makes the barren womb bring forth life.

As we follow the barren womb in the Bible, we see a message that God can make what is dead alive! The barren wombs in the Bible eventually bring forth a child that will be a blessing for many souls because with God, it is all about souls.

Before Sarah was a mother of nations, she was barren.

But Sarai was barren; she *had* no child. Genesis 11:30

And God said unto Abraham, As for Sarai thy wife, thou shalt not call her name Sarai, but Sarah shall her name be. And I will bless her, and give thee a son also of her: yea, I will bless her, and she shall be a mother of nations; kings of people shall be of her. Genesis 17:15-16

Before Rebekah gave birth to Jacob and Esau, she was barren.

And Isaac intreated the LORD for his wife, because she was barren: and the LORD was intreated of him, and Rebekah his wife conceived. And the children struggled together within her; and she said, If it be so, why am I thus? And she went to inquire of the LORD. And the LORD said unto her, Two nations are in thy womb, and two manner of people shall be separated from thy bowels; and the one people shall be stronger than the other people; and the elder shall serve the younger. And when her days to be delivered were fulfilled, behold, there were twins in her womb. Genesis 25:21-24

Before Jacob had the sons of his old age by his wife Rachel, she was barren at first.

And when the LORD saw that Leah *was* hated, he opened her womb: but Rachel *was* barren. Genesis 29:31

And Jacob's anger was kindled against Rachel: and he said, *Am* I in God's stead, who hath withheld from thee the fruit of the womb? And God remembered Rachel, and God hearkened to her, and opened her womb. Genesis 30:2,22

The sons of Rachel; Joseph, and Benjamin: Genesis 35:24

Before Manoah's wife gave birth to mighty Samson, she was barren. Samson would deliver Israel out of the hands of the Phillistines, but at first, his mother was barren.

And there was a certain man of Zorah, of the family of the Danites, whose name was Manoah; and his wife was barren, and bare not. And the angel of the LORD appeared unto the woman, and said unto her, Behold now, thou art barren, and bearest not: but thou shalt conceive, and bear a son. Now therefore beware, I pray thee, and drink not wine nor strong drink, and eat not any unclean thing: For, lo, thou shalt conceive, and bear a son; and no rasor shall come on his head: for the child shall be a Nazarite unto God from the womb: and he shall begin to deliver Israel out of the hand of the Philistines. Judges 13:2-5

Before Hannah gave birth to the great prophet, Samuel who would anoint King David, (1 Samuel 16:12) she was barren.

But unto Hannah he gave a worthy portion; for he loved Hannah: but the LORD had shut up her womb...And they rose up in the morning early, and worshipped before the LORD, and returned, and came to their house to Ramah: and Elkanah knew Hannah his wife; and the LORD remembered her....Wherefore it came to pass, when the time was come about after Hannah had conceived, that she bare a son, and called his name Samuel, saying, Because I have asked him of the LORD. 1 Samuel 1:5,19, 20

Before Elisabeth gave birth to the great messenger, John the Baptist, she was barren.

Verily I say unto you, Among them that are born of women there hath not risen a greater than John the Baptist: . . .Matthew 11:11

And they had no child, because that Elisabeth was barren, and they both were now well stricken in years. . . And there appeared unto him an angel of the Lord standing on the right side of the altar of incense. And when Zacharias saw him, he was troubled, and fear fell upon him. But the angel said unto him, Fear not, Zacharias: for thy prayer is heard; and thy wife Elisabeth shall bear thee a son, and thou shalt call his name John. And thou shalt have joy and gladness; and many shall rejoice at his birth. For he shall be great in the sight of the Lord, and shall drink neither wine nor strong drink; and he shall be filled with the Holy Ghost, even from his mother's womb. And many of the children of Israel shall he turn to the Lord their God. And he shall go before him in the spirit and power of Elias, to turn the hearts of the fathers to the children, and the disobedient to the wisdom of the just; to make ready a people prepared for the Lord. Luke 1:7-17

We have been looking at the barren wombs of women and the children born became great blessings. Now we will look at the most blessed womb of all for it carried our Savior, who came to save the world.

Mary's womb was not barren. She conceived our Lord in her virgin womb. She did so by the power of the Holy Spirit of God. Jesus Christ was not conceived by the seed of man, but by the seed of a woman and the seed of God. He was sinless at birth.

And in the sixth month the angel Gabriel was sent from God unto a city of Galilee, named Nazareth, To a virgin espoused to a man whose name was Joseph, of the house of David; and the virgin's name was Mary. And the angel came in unto her, and said, Hail, thou that art highly favoured, the Lord is with thee: blessed art thou among women. And when she saw him, she was troubled at his saying, and cast in her mind what manner of salutation this should be. And the angel said unto her, Fear not, Mary: for thou hast found favour with God. And, behold, thou shalt conceive in thy womb, and bring forth a son, and shalt call his name JESUS. . . And the angel answered and said unto her, The Holy Ghost shall come upon thee, and the power of the Highest shall overshadow thee: therefore also that holy thing which shall be born of thee shall be called the Son of God. Luke 1:26-35

Now let us look at the spiritual aspect of barrenness and blessedness. Before Christ, our souls are barren of God's life, after Christ they are blessed with God's life. Before Christ we were without God in this world.

That at that time ye were without Christ, being aliens from the commonwealth of Israel, and strangers from the covenants of promise, having no hope, and without God in the world: But now in Christ Jesus ye who sometimes were far off are made nigh by the blood of Christ. Ephesians 2:12-13

We are given eternal life by receiving the word of Life in our hearts.

That which was from the beginning, which we have heard, which we have seen with our eyes, which we have looked upon, and our hands have handled, of the Word of life; (For the life was manifested, and we have seen it, and bear witness, and shew unto you that eternal life, which was with the Father, and was manifested unto us;) 1 John 1:1-2

Christ followers give birth to Christ followers by sharing God's love-truth. The apostles are examples of that.

Then Peter said unto them, Repent, and be baptized every one of you in the name of Jesus Christ for the remission of sins, and ye shall receive the gift of the Holy Ghost. For the promise is unto you, and to your children, and to all that are afar off, even as many as the Lord our God shall call. And with many other words did he testify and exhort, saying, Save yourselves from this untoward generation. Then they that gladly received his word were baptized: and the same day there were added unto them about three thousand souls. Acts 2:38-41

JESUS CHRIST LIGHT

Wherefore, my brethren, ye also are become dead to the law by the body of Christ; that ye should be MARRIED to another, *even* to him who is raised from the dead, that we should BRING FORTH FRUIT unto God. Romans 7:4

BROTHER AND SISTER KEEPERS

It takes great love to keep sheep. It takes great love to be our brother and our sister's keeper.

We will not keep what we do not want; we will only keep what we want.

For instance, if we love God, we will keep God's Word.

Jesus answered and said unto him, If a man love me, he will keep my words: and my Father will love him, and we will come unto him, and make our abode with him. He that loveth me not keepeth not my sayings: and the word which ye hear is not mine, but the Father's which sent me. John 14:23-24

If we keep God's Word and do what it says, His love will mature in us so we can be our brother and sister's keeper in that we look out for them, we encourage them, we are there for them according to God's word. Doing what God says makes us mature in His love.

Cain was not his brother's keeper because Cain didn't keep God's word. We know he didn't keep God's word because God did not respect his offering. Cain hated his brother and he killed his brother, and then he said to God, *Am I my brother's keeper? Genesis 4:9*

Cain said this to God because Cain did not want the responsibility of being his brother's keeper because Cain did not love his brother.

. . .Abel was a keeper of sheep, but Cain was a tiller of the ground. And in process of time it came to pass, that Cain brought of the fruit of the ground an offering unto the Lord. And Abel, he also brought of the firstlings of his flock and of the fat thereof. And the Lord had respect unto Abel and to his offering: But unto Cain and to his offering he had not respect. And Cain was very wroth, and his countenance fell. Genesis 4:2-5

Abel was a keeper of sheep and brought God the first of his flock. That was a real sacrifice for he probably had grown very fond of that sheep, and the sheep was a live offering as well.

God chose many good shepherds of sheep to shepherd His people.

King David was a keeper of sheep before he shepherded God's people as king. He was a man after God's own heart, and God's heart is for people.

He chose David also his servant, and took him from the sheepfolds: From following the ewes great with young he brought him to feed Jacob his people, and Israel his inheritance. Psalm 78:70-71

David stood up for God and for God's people against a giant. He had the courage to do this because he developed great love and faith for his God. His God had been there for him in the sheepfolds, and he knew he would be with him in the battlefields.

David said unto Saul, Thy servant kept his father's sheep, and there came a lion, and a bear, and took a lamb out of the flock: And I went out after him, and smote him, and delivered it out of his mouth: and when he arose against me, I caught him by his beard, and smote him, and slew him. Thy servant slew both the lion and the bear: and this uncircumcised Philistine shall be as one of them, seeing he hath defied the armies of the living God.

David said moreover, The LORD that delivered me out of the paw of the lion, and out of the paw of the bear, he will deliver me out of the hand of this Philistine. And Saul said unto David, Go, and the LORD be with thee. 1 Samuel 17:34-37

Let us see what happens when a shepherd boy with a great big heart stands against a great big giant with no heart.

. . .And the Philistine said unto David, Am I a dog, that thou comest to me with staves? And the Philistine cursed David by his gods. And the Philistine said to David, Come to me, and I will give thy flesh unto the fowls of the air, and to the beasts of the field. Then said David to the Philistine, Thou comest to me with a sword, and with a spear, and with a shield: but I come to thee in the name of the LORD of hosts, the God of the armies of Israel, whom thou hast defied. This day will the LORD deliver thee into mine hand; and I will smite thee, and take thine head from thee; and I will give the carcases of the host of the Philistines this day unto the fowls of the air, and to the wild beasts of the earth; that all the earth may know that there is a God in Israel. And all this assembly shall know that the LORD saveth not with sword and spear: for the battle is the LORD's, and he will give you into our hands. And it came to pass, when the Philistine arose, and came, and drew nigh to meet David, that David hastened, and ran toward the army to meet the Philistine. And David put his hand in his bag, and took thence a stone, and slang it, and smote the Philistine in his forehead, that the stone sunk into his forehead; and he fell upon his face to the earth. So David prevailed over the Philistine with a sling and with a stone, and smote the Philistine, and slew him; but there was no sword in the hand of David. Therefore David ran, and stood upon the Philistine, and took his sword, and drew it out of the sheath thereof, and slew him, and cut off his head therewith. And when the Philistines saw their champion was dead, they fled. 1 Samuel 17:41-51

When David threw that little stone in the name of his big God, that enemy of God's people came down! And David did many mighty things in the name of his Lord.

David is mentioned in Hebrews, chapter eleven.

And what shall I more say? for the time would fail me to tell of Gedeon, and of Barak, and of Samson, and of Jephthae; of David also, and Samuel, and of the prophets: Who through faith subdued kingdoms, wrought righteousness, obtained promises, stopped the mouths of lions. Quenched the violence of fire, escaped the edge of the sword, out of weakness were made strong, waxed valiant in fight, turned to flight the armies of the aliens. 32-34

Moses fled Egypt because his heart was always with his people, God's people. He was raised in Egypt, but he knew who his people were.

And it came to pass in those days, when Moses was grown, that he went out unto his brethren, and looked on their burdens: and he spied an Egyptian smiting an Hebrew, one of his brethren. And he looked this way and that way, and when he saw that there was no man, he slew the Egyptian, and hid him in the sand. And when he went out the second day, behold, two men of the Hebrews strove together: and he said to him that did the wrong, Wherefore smitest thou thy fellow? And he said, Who made thee a prince and a judge over us? intendest thou to kill me, as thou killedst the Egyptian? And Moses feared, and said, Surely this thing is known. Now when Pharaoh heard this thing, he sought to slay Moses. But Moses fled from the face of Pharaoh, and dwelt in the land of Midian: Exodus 2:11-15

While keeping his father in law's flock one day, God called him from the burning bush.

Now Moses kept the flock of Jethro his father in law, the priest of Midian: and he led the flock to the backside of the desert, and came to the mountain of God, even to Horeb. And the angel of the LORD appeared unto him in a flame of fire out of the midst of a bush: and he looked, and, behold, the bush burned with fire, and the bush was not consumed. Exodus 3:1-2

God told him.

Come now therefore, and I will send thee unto Pharaoh, that thou mayest bring forth my people the children of Israel out of Egypt. Exodus 3:10

So, Moses went to Egypt with his shepherd's rod in his hand, which had now been transformed into the rod of God.

And Moses took his wife and his sons, and set them upon an ass, and he returned to the land of Egypt: and Moses took the rod of God in his hand. And the Lord said unto Moses, When thou goest to return into Egypt, see that thou do all those wonders before Pharaoh, which I have put in thine hand: but I will harden his heart, that he shall not let the people go. Exodus 4:20-21

Moses is also mentioned in Hebrews, chapter eleven.

By faith Moses, when he was come to years, refused to be called the son of Pharaoh's daughter; Choosing rather to suffer affliction with the people of God, than to enjoy the pleasures of sin for a season; Esteeming the reproach of Christ greater riches than the treasures in Egypt: for he had respect unto the recompence of the reward. By faith he forsook

Egypt, not fearing the wrath of the king: for he endured, as seeing him who is invisible. Through faith he kept the Passover, and the sprinkling of blood, lest he that destroyed the firstborn should touch them. By faith they passed through the Red sea as by dry land: which the Egyptians assaying to do were drowned. 23-29

Jesus is THE Good Shepherd.

The Good Shepherd lays down His life for the sheep. No man takes His life from Him, He has power to lay it down and He has power to take it again for this is the commandment He received of His Father. He will not leave the sheep when the wolf comes for them for the wolf will scatter them and the wolf will catch them. John 10:11-18 *summarized*

Here is a beautiful prayer in the Bible, about the Great Shepherd of the sheep.

Now may the God who brought us peace by raising from the dead our Lord Jesus Christ so that he would be the Great Shepherd of his flock; and by the power of the blood of the eternal covenant may he work perfection into every part of you giving you all that you need to fulfill your destiny. And may he express through you all that is excellent and pleasing to him through your life-union with Jesus the Anointed One who is to receive all glory forever! Amen! Hebrews 13:20-21 TPT

And God gives us under shepherds. Under shepherds are pastors that keep God's children in various congregations here on earth. A good pastor loves his congregation. They are like the Good Shepherd in many ways.

Psalm 23 is about how the Lord is my Good Shepherd. Let us apply the things that make the Lord, my Good Shepherd with what can make a pastor a good pastor.

Their sheep shall not want.

They make them lie down in green pastures

They lead them beside the still waters.

They restore their souls

They lead them in the paths of righteousness for His name's sake.

Though they walk through the valley of the shadow of death, they will fear no evil, for they are with them and they comfort them

They prepare a table before them in the presence of their enemies

They anoint their head with oil

Their cup runs over

Surely goodness and mercy will follow them all the days of their lives and they will dwell in the house of the Lord forever Psalm 23 NKJV

Paul warns church elders about wolves entering in among the flock to pull them away

Take heed therefore unto yourselves, and to all the flock, over the which the Holy Ghost hath made you overseers, to feed the church of God, which he hath purchased with his own blood. For I know this, that after my departing shall grievous wolves enter in among you, not sparing the flock. Also of your own selves shall men arise, speaking perverse things, to draw away disciples after them.. . .Acts 20:28-30

Peter exhorted the elders.

To the elders among you, I appeal as a fellow elder and a witness of Christ's sufferings who also will share in the glory to be revealed: Be shepherds of God's flock that is under your care, watching over them—not because you must, but because you are willing, as God wants you to be; not pursuing dishonest gain, but eager to serve; not lording it over those entrusted to you, but being examples to the flock. And when the Chief Shepherd appears, you will receive the crown of glory that will never fade away.1 Peter 5:1-4 NIV

JESUS CHRIST LIGHT

The Lord is thy keeper:. . .Psalm 121:5

THE COATS AND THE LOVE

When we follow coats in the Bible, we can see a message of great love. God loves His creation. For instance, He gave all animals a perfect coat. For those living in cold climate, He covered them with a warm coat. For those that might need to blend in, He gave them a coat that would do that. All the animals have the right coat for their temperature and surroundings. This is perfect love.

God made coats for Adam and Eve. Adam knew God's love-truth before the fall. He had knowledge of good and spoke good things and whenever God presented him with something new, he knew how to name it.

. . .and whatsoever Adam called every living creature, that was the name thereof. Genesis 2:19

I believe God recorded the following statement made by Adam so we could get a glimpse into Adam's thought life before the fall. He thought of man and woman together as one flesh.

And Adam said, This is now bone of my bones, and flesh of my flesh: she shall be called Woman, because she was taken out of Man. Therefore shall a man leave his father and his mother, and shall cleave unto his wife: and they shall be one flesh. Genesis 2:23-24

What Adam said about man and woman together is repeated in the New Testament where Paul wrote about the a great mystery of Christ and the Church.

For this cause shall a man leave his father and mother, and shall be joined unto his wife, and they two shall be one flesh. This is a great mystery: but I speak concerning Christ and the church. Ephesians 5:31-32

After believing the lie and falling into sin, the man did not seem to have God's love-truth to cover the woman, and they both ended up in the same predicament, naked and afraid. The same man that had said... *bone of my bones, flesh of my flesh*, did not know what to do. He ran and hid from God and took the woman with him.

After they sinned, Adam and Eve devised their own cover up. They sewed fig leaves together, and made themselves aprons and hid among the trees. . . *camouflage*!

And the eyes of them both were opened, and they knew that they were naked; and they sewed fig leaves together, and made themselves aprons. Genesis 3:7

Blending in with their surroundings to hide from God was not a good plan, nor were the flimsy fig leaves they put together to cover themselves. God covered them better.

Unto Adam also and to his wife did the LORD God make coats of skins, and clothed them. Genesis 3:21

Joseph's father gifted him with a special coat. The coat expressed his father's great love for him because he was the son of his old age.

Now Israel loved Joseph more than all his children, because he *was* the son of his old age: and he made him a coat of *many* colours. And when his brethren saw that their father loved him more than all his brethren, they hated him, and could not speak peaceably unto him. Genesis 37:3-4

Joseph's brothers were jealous of him because of what that coat represented, and they sold him into Egypt. But before they sold him into Egypt, they took his coat off of him and dipped it in blood.

And they took Joseph's coat, and killed a kid of the goats, and dipped the coat in the blood; And they sent the coat of many colours, and they brought it to their father; and said, This have we found: know now whether it be thy son's coat or no. And he knew it, and said, It is my son's coat; an evil beast hath devoured him; Joseph is without doubt rent in pieces. And Jacob rent his clothes, and put sackcloth upon his loins, and mourned for his son many days. Genesis 37:31-34

There is another little coat in the Bible that you may not remember. Hannah loved her son, Samuel. She made a little coat for him that she brought to him from year by year when they went for the yearly sacrifice. Hannah prayed to God for a child and God blessed her with Samuel and after she gave birth to him, she gave him back to the Lord to do the Lord's service all his life.

For this child I prayed; and the LORD hath given me my petition which I asked of him: Therefore also I have lent him to the LORD; as long as he liveth he shall be lent to the LORD. . .1 Samuel 1:27-28

Moreover his mother made him a little coat, and brought it to him from year to year, when she came up with her husband to offer the yearly sacrifice. And Eli blessed Elkanah and his wife, and said, The LORD give thee seed of this woman for the loan which is lent to the LORD. And they went unto their own home. And the LORD visited Hannah, so that she conceived, and bare three sons and two daughters. And the child Samuel grew before the LORD.1 Samuel 2:19-21

Shadrach, Meshach, and Abed-nego were thrown in the fiery furnace, but the fire didn't touch the coats they had on. The three would not bow to the golden image erected by king Nebuchadnezzar so they were thrown into the fiery furnace. But God covered them from the flames. God was with them in the fire.

And these three men, Shadrach, Meshach, and Abednego, fell down bound into the midst of the burning fiery furnace. Then Nebuchadnezzar the king was astonied, and rose up in haste, and spake, and said unto his counsellors, Did not we cast three men bound into the midst of the fire? They answered and said unto the king, True, O king. He answered and said, Lo, I see four men loose, walking in the midst of the fire, and they have no hurt; and the form of the fourth is like the Son of God. Then Nebuchadnezzar came near to the mouth of the burning fiery furnace, and spake, and said, Shadrach, Meshach, and Abednego, ye servants of the most high God, come forth, and come hither. Then Shadrach, Meshach, and Abednego, came forth of the midst of the fire. And the princes, governors, and captains, and the king's counsellors, being gathered together, saw these men, upon whose bodies the fire had no power, nor was an hair of their head singed, neither were their coats changed, nor the smell of fire had passed on them. Daniel 3:23-27

Jesus told about a prodigal son that returned home to his father after wasting away his inheritance. His father loved him and immediately sent for him the best robe.

Bring forth the best robe, and put it on him; and put a ring on his hand, and shoes on his feet: And bring hither the fatted calf, and kill it; and let us eat, and be merry: For this my son was dead, and is alive again; he was lost, and is found. And they began to be merry. Luke 15:11-24

Our sins our covered by the blood of Jesus because of God's great love for us.

What happy fulfillment is ahead for those whose rebellion has been forgiven and whose sins are covered by blood. What happy progress comes to them when they hear the Lord speak over them, "I will never hold your sins against you!" Romans 4:7-8 TPT

We are born into this world naked, and just like God did for Adam and Eve, God wants to cover us with His love. God's love is the love the world cannot give us, and it is a love the world can't take away from us. But without God's love-truth, people look for love in all the wrong places.

And throughout our lives, we will see the love of God covering over others, and we will either love it or hate it; we will either want it or we will push it away.

JESUS CHRIST LIGHT

Jesus was stripped of His coat so God could cover us with His love. The coat Jesus had on the day He was crucified was a sturdy coat, it was without seam, woven from the top throughout. Unlike the many kinds of loves we may encounter in this life, God's love is like that coat, hard to rend and weaves its way beautifully in our hearts.

. . .now the coat was without seam, woven from the top throughout. They said therefore among themselves, Let us not rend it, but cast lots for it. . John 19:23-24

THE FEET AND THE AUTHORITY

When we follow feet in the Bible, we can see a message of authority, authority of God's love. If we consider natural feet, we can better understand spiritual feet. Natural feet are the lowest point of the body. After the feet, there is no more body. Anything below the feet is below the body and the body is above whatever is below the feet.

The devil is referred to as a serpent. And a serpent has no feet. The serpent has no real authority.

After the fall of mankind, God sent the serpent upon his belly to eat dust. He became the lowest of the low by the judgment of God.

There are some amazing feet in the Bible. Moses' feet took him on a journey to deliver God's people.

God told Moses to take the shoes off his feet while in His presence at the burning bush. It was there that God gave Moses a holy mission for his feet.

God called unto him out of the midst of the bush, and said, Moses, Moses. And he said, Here am I. And he said, Draw not nigh hither: put off thy shoes from off thy feet, for the place whereon thou standest is holy ground. Moreover he said, I am the God of thy father, the God of Abraham, the God of Isaac, and the God of Jacob. And Moses hid his face; for he was afraid to look upon God. And the LORD said, I have surely seen the affliction of my people which are in Egypt, and have heard their cry by reason of their taskmasters; for I know their sorrows; And I am come down to deliver them out of the hand of the Egyptians, and to bring them up out of that land unto a good land. . . .Come now therefore, and I will send thee unto Pharaoh, that thou mayest bring forth my people the children of Israel out of Egypt. Exodus 3:4-10

The children of Israel ate their first Passover with their shoes on their feet because they were about to be loosed by the power of God Almighty.

At the first Passover, they ate with their shoes on because they were about to take a journey in a hurry. God was about to show who was in control and they were about to be let go.

And thus shall ye eat it; *with* your loins girded, *your shoes on your feet*, and your staff in your hand; and ye shall eat it in haste: it *is* the LORD'S Passover. Exodus 12:11

A very important marriage takes place in the Book of Ruth. Before Ruth and Boaz get married, at the direction of her mother in law, Ruth places herself at the feet of Boaz.

Her mother in law told her.

Wash thyself therefore, and anoint thee, and put thy raiment upon thee, and get thee down to the floor: but make not thyself known unto the man, until he shall have done eating and drinking. And it shall be, when he lieth down, that thou shalt mark the place where he shall lie, and thou shalt go in, and uncover his feet, and lay thee down; and he will tell thee what thou shalt do. Ruth 3:3-4

And when Boaz had eaten and drunk, and his heart was merry, he went to lie down at the end of the heap of corn: and she came softly, and uncovered his feet, and laid her down And it came to pass at midnight, that the man was afraid, and turned himself: and, behold, a woman lay at his feet. Ruth 3:7-8

We know they got married and Ruth gave birth to Obed who later had Jesse who is the father of David. Ruth 4:17-22

The greatest gift for mankind, Jesus Christ, the One who would put death under His feet came from that family tree. Matthew 1:1

Forgiving a person for something they did against us is like a lender having the authority to forgive a large debt. And just as the lender has the authority to cast a debtor in jail, when a person holds something over another person it's like putting them in jail!

Then Jesus told of a king who forgave a servant a very large debt, but that same servant would not forgive his fellow servant, who owed him a lesser debt.

But the same servant went out, and found one of his fellowservants, which owed him an hundred pence: and he laid hands on him, and took him by the throat, saying, Pay me that thou owest. And his fellowservant *fell down at his feet*, and besought him, saying, Have patience with me, and I will pay thee all. Matthew 18:28-29

When the king found out that the one he had forgiven had not forgiven his fellowman, he called him to him and said.

O thou wicked servant, I forgave thee all that debt, because thou desiredst me: Shouldest not thou also have had compassion on thy fellowservant, even as I had pity on thee? And his lord was wroth, and delivered him to the tormentors, till he should pay all that was due unto him. So likewise shall my heavenly Father do also unto you, if ye from your hearts forgive not every one his brother their trespasses. Matthew 18:32-35

The woman with the alabaster box knew Jesus was Lord and Christ. She washed his feet with her tears and wiped them with the hairs of her head. She kissed His feet. She anointed His feet with ointment.

And *stood at his feet* behind *him* weeping, and began to wash his *feet* with tears, and did wipe *them* with the hairs of her head, and *kissed his feet*, and anointed *them* with the ointment. . . And he turned to the woman, and said unto Simon, Seest thou this woman? I entered into thine house, thou gavest me no water for my feet: but she hath washed my feet with tears, and wiped *them* with the hairs of her head. . . Thou gavest me no kiss: but this woman since the time I came in hath not ceased to kiss my feet.. . My head with oil thou didst not anoint: but this woman hath anointed my feet with ointment. Luke 7:38, 44, 45, 46

Jesus Christ has authority over sickness. When they cast the sick at the feet of Jesus, they were acknowledging His authority to heal them.

And great multitudes came unto him, having with them *those that were* lame, blind, dumb, maimed, and many others, and cast them down at Jesus' feet; and he healed them: Matthew 15:30

Jesus has authority over devils.

Then they went out to see what was done; and came to Jesus, and found the man, out of whom the devils were departed, *sitting at the feet* of Jesus, clothed, and in his right mind: and they were afraid. Luke 8:35

At the last supper, Jesus was about to be crucified and He knew He would be going away. When He washed his disciples feet, He was telling them to love one another as He had loved them. He loved them by teaching them, encouraging them, comforting them, being patient with them, correcting them, challenging them, and forgiving them.

So after he had washed their feet, and had taken his garments, and was set down again, he said unto them, Know ye what I have done to you? Ye call me Master and Lord: and ye say well; for so I am. If I then, your Lord and Master, have washed your feet; ye also ought to wash one another's feet. For I have given you an example, that ye should do as I have done to you. Verily, verily, I say unto you, The servant is not greater than his lord; neither he that is sent greater than he that sent him. If ye know these things, happy are ye if ye do them. . . A new commandment I give unto you, That ye love one another; as I have loved you, that ye also love one another. By this shall all men know that ye are my disciples, if ye have love one to another. John 13:12-17; 34-35

In the New Testament, the feet of Jesus were first mentioned by John the Baptist when John said he wasn't worthy of Christ's shoes. John told the people Christ was mightier than he was, for He had the authority to baptize them in the Holy Ghost and fire.

I indeed baptize you with water unto repentance: but he that cometh after me is mightier than I, *whose shoes I am not worthy to bear:* he shall baptize you with the Holy Ghost, and *with* fire: Matthew 3:11

Jesus has authority on earth to forgive sins.

And, behold, men brought in a bed a man which was taken with a palsy: and they sought means to bring him in, and to lay him before him. And when they could not find by what way they might bring him in because of the multitude, they went upon the housetop, and let him down through the tiling with his couch into the midst before Jesus. And when he saw their faith, he said unto him, Man, thy sins are forgiven thee. And the scribes and the Pharisees began to reason, saying, Who is this which speaketh blasphemies? Who can forgive sins, but God alone?

But when Jesus perceived their thoughts, he answering said unto them, What reason ye in your hearts? Whether is easier, to say, Thy sins be forgiven thee; or to say, Rise up and walk? But that ye may know that the Son of man hath power upon earth to forgive sins, (he said unto the sick of the palsy,) I say unto thee, Arise, and take up thy couch, and go into thine house. And immediately he rose up before them, and took up that whereon he lay, and departed to his own house, glorifying God. Luke 5:18-25

When mankind falls at the feet of Jesus for forgiveness, He has the power to forgive them. When mankind falls at our feet for forgiveness, we have the power to forgive them in Jesus' Name. And being unforgiving is really not an option for a Christian.

And forgive us our debts, as we forgive our debtors. Matthew 6:12

Jesus Christ has the authority over death. When Mary, the sister of Lazarus, fell at the feet of Jesus, it was signifying that authority.

She fell *down at his feet*, saying, Lord, if thou hadst been here, my brother had not died. John 11:21

Jesus told her.

I am the resurrection, and the life: he that believeth in me, though he were dead, yet shall he live: And whosoever liveth and believeth in me shall never die. Believest thou this? She saith unto him, Yea, Lord: I believe that thou art the Christ, the Son of God, which should come into the world. (25-27)

And when He raised her brother back to life, He demonstrated His authority even over death!

And when he thus had spoken, he cried with a loud voice, Lazarus, come forth. And he that was dead came forth, bound hand and foot with graveclothes: and his face was bound about with a napkin. Jesus saith unto them, Loose him, and let him go. John 11:43-44

The gospel of Jesus Christ is the power of God unto salvation. It is God's love-truth that has the authority to save, and the authority to raise!

For I am not ashamed of the gospel of Christ: for it is the power of God unto salvation to every one that believeth; to the Jew first, and also to the Greek. Romans 1:16

And the Bible mentions the beautiful feet. Feet that carry God's love-truth, the gospel of Jesus Christ. When we bring this good news to people, we are bringing the power and authority of God to save them.

How then shall they call on him in whom they have not believed? and how shall they believe in him of whom they have not heard? and how shall they hear without a preacher? And how shall they preach, except they be sent? as it is written, How beautiful are the feet of them that preach the gospel of peace, and bring glad tidings of good things! Romans 10:14-15

JESUS CHRIST LIGHT

Then cometh the end, when he shall have delivered up the kingdom to God, even the Father; when he shall have put down all rule and all authority and power. For he must reign, till he hath put all enemies under his feet. The last enemy that shall be destroyed is death. . .1 Corinthians 15:24-28

FACE TO FACE AND THE REVEAL

Whenever we see a face to face encounter with God in the Bible, we can see a reveal.

When Jacob came face to face with God, his new name was revealed to him and why it was given him.

Jacob had taken his family from his father in law Laban's house. Laban caught up with him and was upset that he left like that. After they sorted things out and Laban departed from Jacob and his family, Jacob started on his way again.

As he did, angels of God came to meet him. When Jacob saw them, he exclaimed, "This is God's camp!" So he named the place Mahanaim.

Jacob was on his way to meet his brother Esau who had sold his birthright to him and he was afraid about the encounter, so he prayed.

"O God of my father Abraham and God of my father Isaac, the Lord who said to me, 'Return to your country and to your family, and I will deal well with you': I am not worthy of the least of all the mercies and of all the truth which You have shown Your servant; for I crossed over this Jordan with my staff, and now I have become two companies. Deliver me, I pray, from the hand of my brother, from the hand of Esau; for I fear him, lest he come and attack me and the mother with the children. For You said, 'I will surely treat you well, and make your descendants as the sand of the sea, which cannot be numbered for multitude.'

Jacob sent his servants ahead with presents, along with his two wives, their two women servants, and his eleven sons.

Then Jacob was left alone; and a Man wrestled with him until the breaking of day. Now when He saw that He did not prevail against him, He touched the socket of his hip; and the socket of Jacob's hip was out of joint as He wrestled with him. And He said, "Let Me go, for the day breaks." But he said, "I will not let You go unless You bless me!" So He said to him, "What is your name?" He said, "Jacob." And He said, "Your name shall no longer be called Jacob, but Israel; for you have struggled with God and with men, and have prevailed." Then Jacob asked, saying, "Tell me Your name, I pray." And He said, "Why is it that you ask about My name?" And He blessed him there. So Jacob called the name of the place Peniel: "For I have seen God face to face, and my life is preserved. Read Genesis 31 and 32

Jacob's new name, Israel was revealed to him because he had struggled with God and with men, and prevailed. The name Israel means, *God prevails*.

Moses desired God's presence to go with the people wherever they would go. The Lord spoke to Moses face to face as a man speaks to a friend. God knew his name.

And the Lord spake unto Moses face to face, as a man speaketh unto his friend. . .

And Moses said to God, If thy presence go not with me, carry us not up hence. For wherein shall it be known here that I and thy people have found grace in thy sight? is it not in that thou goest with us? so shall we be separated, I and thy people, from all the people that are upon the face of the earth. And the Lord said unto Moses, I will do this thing also that thou hast spoken: for thou hast found grace in my sight, and I know thee by name. And he said, I beseech thee, shew me thy glory. And he said, I will make all my goodness pass before thee, and I will proclaim the name of the LORD before thee; Exodus 33:11-19

And the Lord revealed to Moses His goodness. And all the Lord's goodness passed before Moses and He proclaimed the name of the Lord.

And the LORD descended in the cloud, and stood with him there, and proclaimed the name of the LORD. And the LORD passed by before him, and proclaimed, The LORD, The LORD God, merciful and gracious, longsuffering, and abundant in goodness and truth,

Keeping mercy for thousands, forgiving iniquity and transgression and sin, and that will by no means clear the guilty; visiting the iniquity of the fathers upon the children, and upon the children's children, unto the third and to the fourth generation. Exodus 34:5-7

The God's love-truth is like a mirror. We look into it and see what God wants us to see and it's only a peek, but that peek is wonderful! One day, we will see as clearly as He already sees us. We will know even as we are known.

Love is very patient and kind, never jealous or envious, never boastful or proud, never haughty or selfish or rude. Love does not demand its own way. It is not irritable or touchy. It does not hold grudges and will hardly even notice when others do it wrong. It is never glad about injustice, but rejoices whenever truth wins out. If you love someone, you will be loyal to him no matter what the cost. You will always believe in him, always expect the best of him, and always stand your ground in defending him. All the special gifts and powers from God will someday come to an end, but love goes on forever. Someday prophecy and speaking in unknown languages and special knowledge—these gifts will disappear. Now we know so little, even with our special gifts, and the preaching of those most gifted is still so poor. But when we have been made perfect and complete, then the need for these inadequate special gifts will come to an end, and they will disappear. It's like this: when I was a child I spoke and thought and reasoned as a child does. But when I became a man my thoughts grew far beyond those of my childhood, and now I have put away the childish things. In the same way, we can see and understand only a little about God now, as if we were peering at his reflection in a poor mirror; but someday we are going to see him in his completeness, face-to-face. Now all that I know is hazy and blurred, but then I will see everything clearly, just as clearly as God sees into my heart right now. There are three things that remain—faith, hope, and love—and the greatest of these is love. 1 Corinthians 13:4-13 TLB

When we turn to the Lord Jesus, the Spirit of God reveals His glory to us. We become mirrors of who He is and who we are in Him as we walk in God's love-truth.

But whenever someone turns to the Lord, the veil is taken away. For the Lord is the Spirit, and wherever the Spirit of the Lord is, there is freedom. So all of us who have had that veil removed can see and reflect the glory of the Lord. And the Lord—who is the Spirit—makes us more and more like him as we are changed into his glorious image. 2 Corinthians 3:16-18 NLT

James wrote about how hearing God's love-truth and not doing it is like looking in a mirror then walking away and forgetting what we look like, but if we obey God's love-truth we will be clear on what we are supposed to be doing.

Obey the Word of God. If you hear only and do not act, you are only fooling yourself. Anyone who hears the Word of God and does not obey is like a man looking at his face in a mirror. After he sees himself and goes away, he forgets what he looks like. But the one who keeps looking into God's perfect Law and does not forget it will do what it says and be happy as he does it. God's Word makes men free. If a person thinks he is religious, but does not keep his tongue from speaking bad things, he is fooling himself. His religion is worth nothing. Religion that is pure and good before God the Father is to help children who have no parents and to care for women whose husbands have died who have troubles. Pure religion is also to keep yourself clean from the sinful things of the world. James 1:22-27 NLV

Prayer of David

As for me, I will behold thy face in righteousness: I shall be satisfied, when I awake, with thy likeness. Psalm 17:15

JESUS CHRIST LIGHT:

But if any man love God, the same is known of him. 1 Corinthians 8:3

FINGER OF JUDGMENT

When we go before a judge here, the judge hears the witnesses and weighs the evidence before passing judgment.

Just judgment is a good thing, unjust judgment is a bad thing.

It has never been popular to point out what is evil. If ever the truth hurts, it hurts when it threatens one's ability to do what one wants to do.

On a whole, people do not like being told what to do, or what not to do, or to be judged and we can't blame them because there are a lot of judgmental people out there and what they're saying is not being said in the spirit of love. It is condemning and it is shaming. Love-truth never does that! God's truth is love-truth. It does not tear down, it builds up. When we share truth with people, it should be love-truth.

Judging or weighing what is right and what is wrong by God's Word is always just. The Old Testament was written by Love. The New Testament was written by Love. God is love. When there is love, there is always justice. It is true, there are many things God judges as sin, and sin has to be punished, but in Jesus Christ, love triumphs over judgment! Judging is more than passing a sentence or deciding who is guilty or who is innocent; right or wrong. Judging is making the right calls for the good of all. God always makes the right calls.

When we follow fingers in the Bible, we can see judgment.

Creation is the work of God's fingers, and He balanced it all out perfectly.

When I look at the night sky and see the work of your fingers the moon and the stars you set in place what are mere mortals that you should think about them, human beings that you should care for them? Yet you made them only a little lower than God and crowned them with glory and honor. You gave them charge of everything you made, putting all things under their authority the flocks and the herds and all the wild animals, the birds in the sky, the fish in the sea, and everything that swims the ocean currents. O Lord, our Lord, your majestic name fills the earth! Psalm 8 NLT

When Aaron stretched out the rod of God and did wonders in Egypt it was referred to by the magicians of Pharaoh as the finger of God.

And the Lord said unto Moses, Say unto Aaron, Stretch out thy rod, and smite the dust of the land, that it may become lice throughout all the land of Egypt. And they did so; for Aaron stretched out his hand with his rod, and smote the dust of the earth, and it became lice in man, and in beast; all the dust of the land became lice throughout all the land of Egypt. And the magicians did so with their enchantments to bring forth lice, but they could not: so there were lice upon man, and upon beast. Then the magicians said unto Pharaoh, This is the finger of God: and Pharaoh's heart was hardened, and he hearkened not unto them; as the Lord had said. Exodus 8:16-19

The plagues in Egypt were the judgment of God.

And the Lord said unto Moses, See, I have made thee a god to Pharaoh: and Aaron thy brother shall be thy prophet. Thou shalt speak all that I command thee: and Aaron thy brother shall speak unto Pharaoh, that he send the children of Israel out of his land. And I will harden Pharaoh's heart, and multiply my signs and my wonders in the land of Egypt. But Pharaoh shall not hearken unto you, that I may lay my hand upon Egypt, and bring forth mine armies, and my people the children of Israel, out of the land of Egypt by great judgments. And the Egyptians shall know that I am the Lord, when I stretch forth mine hand upon Egypt, and bring out the children of Israel from among them. Exodus 7:1-5

God wrote the Ten Commandments on tables of stone with His finger. The commandments of God are the judgments of God. They are what He has decided as right and just!

And he gave unto Moses, when he had made an end of communing with him upon mount Sinai, two tables of testimony, tables of stone, written with the finger of God.

Thou shalt have no other gods before me.
Thou shalt not take the name of the LORD thy God in vain
Remember the sabbath day, to keep it holy
Honour thy father and thy mother
Thou shalt not kill.
Thou shalt not commit adultery.
Thou shalt not steal.
Thou shalt not bear false witness against thy neighbour.
Thou shalt not covet Exodus 31:18, 20:3-17

In obedience to God's law, the priests took the blood of the sin offering with their finger and put it on the horns of the altar.

And the priest shall take of the blood of the sin offering with his finger, and put it upon the horns of the altar of burnt offering, and shall pour out his blood at the bottom of the altar of burnt offering. Leviticus 4:25

Daniel interpreted the writing on the wall for King Belshazzar. It was a judgment and it was written with the fingers of a man's hand. Read Daniel 5

Daniel reminded the king what happened to his father Nebuchadnezzar when his heart was lifted up with pride and how he was driven from his kingdom for a time and ate grass like oxen. Belshazzar was lifting himself up against the Lord of heaven by bringing the vessels of God's house into his kingdom and letting people drink from them, and for praising idols and not God.

In the same hour came forth fingers of a man's hand, and wrote over against the candlestick upon the plaister of the wall of the king's palace: and the king saw the part of the hand that wrote.

Then was the part of the hand sent from him; and this writing was written. And this is the writing that was written, MENE, MENE, TEKEL, UPHARSIN. This is the interpretation of the thing: MENE; God hath numbered thy kingdom, and finished it. TEKEL; Thou art weighed in the balances, and art found wanting. 5:24-27

Jesus wrote something on the ground with His finger when they asked Him if they should stone the woman caught in the act of adultery. Jesus came to pronounce life, not death.

And the scribes and Pharisees brought unto him [Jesus] a woman taken in adultery; and when they had set her in the midst, They say unto him, Master, this woman was taken in adultery, in the very act. Now Moses in the law commanded us, that such should be stoned: but what sayest thou? This they said, tempting him, that they might have to accuse him. But Jesus stooped down, and with his finger wrote on the ground, as though he heard them not. So when they continued asking him, he lifted up himself, and said unto them, He that is without sin among you, let him first cast a stone at her. And again he stooped down, and wrote on the ground. And they which heard it, being convicted by their own conscience, went out one by one, beginning at the eldest, even unto the last: and Jesus was left alone, and the woman standing in the midst. When Jesus had lifted up himself, and saw none but the woman, he said unto her, Woman, where are those thine accusers? hath no man condemned thee? She said, No man, Lord. And Jesus said unto her, Neither do I condemn thee: go, and sin no more. John 8:3-11

Jesus was the only one that could have thrown a stone that day because He was the only one without sin, but He didn't throw a stone. He didn't condemn her to death. He told her to go (*live*) and sin no more.

We do not know what Jesus wrote on the ground with His finger that day, but we do know the two greatest commandments and on these two hang all the law and the prophets.

Jesus said unto him, Thou shalt love the Lord thy God with all thy heart, and with all thy soul, and with all thy mind. This is the first and great commandment. And the second is like unto it, Thou shalt love thy neighbour as thyself. On these two commandments hang all the law and the prophets. Matthew 22:37-40

The written Word of God, from Genesis to Revelation, was also written by the finger of God in that it is inspired by God. We should believe the writing in the Word of God! If we are judged by our own ways, we will always be found wanting. If we are judged by our relationship with Jesus, we will never be found wanting. And that's the God's absolute love-truth!

It's not only with our bodies that we can sin against someone, we can sin against them in our thoughts and our hearts. If we keep God's laws just so we will not get into trouble, it's not really just. We must keep God's law because we love God and we love people, that is just. This is what Jesus had to say about that.

"If you think I've come to set aside the law of Moses or the writings of the prophets, you're mistaken. I have come to fulfill and bring to perfection all that has been written. Indeed, I assure you, as long as heaven and earth endure, not even the smallest detail of the Law will be done away with until its purpose is complete. So whoever violates even the least important of the commandments, and teaches others to do so, will be the least esteemed in the realm of heaven's kingdom. But whoever obeys them and teaches their truths to others will be greatly esteemed in the realm of heaven's kingdom. . You're familiar with the commandment, Do not murder or you will be judged. 'But I'm telling you, if you hold anger in your heart toward a fellow believer, you are subject to judgment. . . Your ancestors have been taught, 'Never commit adultery. However, I say to you, if you look with lust in your eyes at the body of a woman who is not your wife, you've already committed adultery in your heart. . ."It has been said, 'Whoever divorces his wife must give her legal divorce papers.' However, I say to you, if anyone divorces his wife for any reason, except for infidelity, he causes her to commit adultery, and whoever marries a divorced woman commits adultery." Matthew 5:17-32 TPT

Here is a brief contrast between the law of Moses and the law of grace. One was governed by death, the other by life.

The Government of Death, its constitution chiseled on stone tablets, had a dazzling inaugural. Moses' face as he delivered the tablets was so bright that day (even though it would fade soon enough) that the people of Israel could no more look right at him than stare into the sun. How much more dazzling, then, the Government of Living Spirit? 2 Corinthians 3:7-8 The Message

In the end, we will be judged by our relationship and identification with Jesus Christ. What we do with the word of God concerning Jesus Christ in this life will be our judge in the afterlife.

He that rejecteth me, and receiveth not my words, hath one that judgeth him: the word that I have spoken, the same shall judge him in the last day. John 12:48

The Holy Spirit convicts the world of sin and righteousness and judgement.

Nevertheless, I tell you the truth: it is to your advantage that I go away, for if I do not go away, the Helper will not come to you. But if I go, I will send him to you. And when he comes, he will convict the world concerning sin and righteousness and judgment: concerning sin, because they do not believe in me; concerning righteousness, because I go to the Father, and you will see me no longer; concerning judgment, because the ruler of this world is judged. John 16:7-11 ESV

Jesus Christ is perfect, we are not! And we will do something that is against God's law from time to time, but Christ is our advocate with the Father, and He pleads our case. Jesus Christ is the righteous one.

My dear children, I am writing this to you so that you will not sin. But if anyone does sin, we have an advocate who pleads our case before the Father. He is Jesus Christ, the one who is truly righteous. He himself is the sacrifice that atones for our sins—and not only our sins but the sins of all the world. 1 John 2:1-2 NLT

In Leviticus, we often see the phrase, *put to death*, when someone has broken the law. Thank God we are no longer under the law in that respect. We now obey the laws of God because of our new life in Christ. Instead of not doing bad because we will be punished under law, we do good because we are not being punished under grace.

None of God's commandments have passed away, they are now written in hearts.

Behold, the days come, saith the Lord, that I will make a new covenant with the house of Israel, and with the house of Judah: Not according to the covenant that I made with their fathers in the day that I took them by the hand to bring them out of the land of Egypt; which my covenant they brake, although I was an husband unto them, saith the Lord : But this shall be the covenant that I will make with the house of Israel; After those days, saith the Lord, I will put my law in their inward parts, and write it in their hearts; and will be their God, and they shall be my people. And they shall teach no more every man his neighbour, and every man his brother, saying, Know the Lord : for they shall all know me, from the least of them unto the greatest of them, saith the Lord : for I will forgive their iniquity, and I will remember their sin no more. Jeremiah 31:31-34

In Christ, we obey God because we love God, not because we fear God. If all of God's commandments were obeyed today, we would be living in a just society.

God is love. If you live in love, you live by the help of God and God lives in you. Love is made perfect in us when we are not ashamed as we stand before Him on the day He judges. For we know that our life in this world is His life lived in us.1 John 4: 16-17 NLV

JESUS CHRIST LIGHT

But if I with the finger of God cast out devils, no doubt the kingdom of God is come upon you. Luke 11:20

THE EYE AND THE OBJECT OF OUR AFFECTION

When we see eyes in the Bible, we can see the object of our affection. What we look at is what we love.

We are the object of God's affection for His eyes run to and fro throughout the whole earth, to shew Himself strong in the behalf of those whose heart is perfect toward Him.

Hanani the seer told Asa king of Judah that the eyes of the Lord look for those He can show Himself strong for, but Asa had been looking to the king of Syria and not the Lord, and so because of that Hanani told Asa he would have wars.

And at that time Hanani the seer came to Asa king of Judah, and said unto him, Because thou hast relied on the king of Syria, and not relied on the LORD thy God, therefore is the host of the king of Syria escaped out of thine hand. Were not the Ethiopians and the Lubims a huge host, with very many chariots and horsemen? yet, because thou didst rely on the LORD, he delivered them into thine hand. For the eyes of the LORD run to and fro throughout the whole earth, to shew himself strong in the behalf of them whose heart is perfect toward him. Herein thou hast done foolishly: therefore from henceforth thou shalt have wars. 2 Chronicles 16:7-9

Sadly, the forbidden tree was the object of Eve's affection.

And when the woman saw that the tree *was* good for food, and that it *was* pleasant to the eyes, and a tree to be desired to make *one* wise, she took of the fruit thereof, and did eat, and gave also unto her husband with her; and he did eat. Genesis 3:6

When the children of Israel were hungry, the fleshpots of Egypt were the object of their affection

And the children of Israel said unto them, Would to God we had died by the hand of the Lord in the land of Egypt, when we sat by the flesh pots, and when we did eat bread to the full; for ye have brought us forth into this wilderness, to kill this whole assembly with hunger. Exodus 16:3

The manna from heaven should have been the object of their affection. They did not see manna as a blessing.

But now our soul *is* dried away: *there is* nothing at all, beside this manna, *before* our eyes. Numbers 11:6

If the love of money is the object of our affection, we have an evil eye. The Bible warns of the evil eye. A greedy person has an evil eye. They are looking at one thing, and that one thing is money, and what money can buy them. And it is the love of money that is the root of all evil. And this is the God's absolute love-truth!

For the love of money is the root of all evil: which while some coveted after, they have erred from the faith, and pierced themselves through with many sorrows. 1 Timothy 6:10

When a person's main focus is the love of money or the love of what money can buy, the light of God's love cannot get through to them. The greed inside of them will not let it in.

For where your treasure is, there will your heart be also. The light of the body is the eye: if therefore thine eye be single, thy whole body shall be full of light. But if thine eye be evil, thy whole body shall be full of darkness. If therefore the light that is in thee be darkness, how great is that darkness!. Matthew 6:21-23

The disciples referred to Jesus as Master. We can only have eyes for one master. God should be the object of our affection, not money.

Jesus taught,

No man can serve two masters: for either he will hate the one, and love the other; or else he will hold to the one, and despise the other. Ye cannot serve God and mammon. Matthew 6:24

Jesus taught that the evil eye comes from the heart.

And he said, That which cometh out of the man, that defileth the man. For from within, out of the heart of men, proceed evil thoughts, adulteries, fornications, murders, thefts, covetousness, wickedness, deceit, lasciviousness, an evil eye, blasphemy, pride, foolishness: All these evil things come from within, and defile the man. Mark 7:20-23

When teaching about the kingdom of heaven, Jesus told about a householder who went out early in the morning and hired laborers to work in his vineyard. At the first hour, he agreed with the first laborers to work for a penny a day. He kept going out at various times throughout the day all the way up to the eleventh hour. He hired more laborers for, *whatsoever was right*, and they all agreed upon that price. But when it was time to pay up, he started with the last ones he hired and worked his way up to the first ones he hired. He gave them all a penny. But the ones who were hired first were upset that the ones that worked only an hour received the same pay they did, who had worked all day long. This is the answer they were given when they demanded their fair share.

. . .Is it not lawful for me to do what I will with mine own? Is thine eye evil, because I am good? Matthew 20: 1-15

The world system is run by money and we know the worth of money fluctuates. The world may say about someone who has a lot of money, that they are worth a lot. Money should never determine one's worth.

Speaking to the people, Jesus continued, "Be alert and guard your heart from greed and always wishing for what you don't have. For your life can never be measured by the amount of things you possess." Luke 12:15 TPT

We can have money and use money for good, but we cannot have love of money for it will hinder us from seeing eternal things....*our eternal God and eternal souls.*

If we have the love of money more than the love of God, it is like sleeping with the enemy. To illustrate, we will look at two types of women mentioned in the Bible: a wife and a harlot.

Being a wife is much better than being a harlot. So, what is the difference between a wife and a harlot?

We look at a wife as the love of a husband's life. It is a commitment.

They become one in all things. They have the same name; they live in the same house; they have the same money; they have the same children; etc...

We see a harlot, on the other hand, as a *one night stand* and the reason for the relationship is for physical pleasure and money. There is no commitment, there is no home, there is no family, there is no love, there is just lust.

A relationship with God is like a marriage.

A relationship with the world is like a one night stand.

When we are in bed with the world, it is like a one night stand, it usually involves pleasure and money. *And we are cheating on God.*

Greed brought Judas down. The bag was the object of his affection for he was a thief. And he ended up selling his soul for thirty pieces of silver.

Then saith one of his disciples, Judas Iscariot, Simon's son, which should betray him, Why was not this ointment sold for three hundred pence, and given to the poor? This he said, not that he cared for the poor; but because he was a thief, and had the bag, and bare what was put therein. John 12:4-6

Then one of the twelve, called Judas Iscariot, went unto the chief priests, And said unto them, What will ye give me, and I will deliver him unto you? And they covenanted with him for thirty pieces of silver. Matthew 26:14-15 KJV

When Jesus walked the earth, souls were the object of His affection. He was moved by compassion by what He saw, and He did something about it.

And Jesus went forth, and saw a great multitude, and was moved with compassion toward them, and he healed their sick. Matthew 14:14

In heaven, souls are still the object of Christ's affection.

For Christ is not entered into the holy places made with hands, which are the figures of the true; but into heaven itself, now to appear in the presence of God for us: Hebrews 9:24

The object of the apostle Paul's affection was souls. He wanted to gain souls for God.

For though I be free from all men, yet have I made myself servant unto all, that I might gain the more. And unto the Jews I became as a Jew, that I might gain the Jews; to them that are under the law, as under the law, that I might gain them that are under the law. To them that are without law, as without law, (being not without law to God, but under the law to Christ,) that I might gain them that are without law. To the weak became I as weak, that I might gain the weak: I am made all things to all men, that I might by all means save some. 1 Corinthians 9:19-22

We should want to save a soul from death and hide a multitude of sins by sharing God's love-truth.

Brethren, if any of you do err from the truth, and one convert him; Let him know, that he which converteth the sinner from the error of his way shall save a soul from death, and shall hide a multitude of sins. James 5:19-20

JESUS CHRIST LIGHT

You can buy two sparrows for only a copper coin, yet not even one sparrow falls from its nest without the knowledge of your Father. Aren't you worth much more to God than many sparrows? 30–31 So don't worry. For your Father cares deeply about even the smallest detail of your life. Matthew 10:29-31 TPT

THE KISSES AND THE INTENTIONS

When a bride marches down the aisle on her wedding day to wed her 'prince', it is one of the happiest days of her life. The last words they hear in the ceremony is directed to the groom; *you may now kiss the bride.*

A long time ago, the first kiss at the wedding may have been the first time the two kissed. The kiss completes the ceremony, seals the deal.

One of my favorite movies is Enchanted. There is a song in that movie I love because it's about true love, *True Love's Kiss.* *"I've been dreaming of a true love's kiss and a prince I'm hoping comes with this"*

This is a fairy tale, but the theme of the movie, true love, is no fairy tale. God is true love. When we invite God into our lives, our lives our kissed by grace for the first time. And this is the God's absolute love-truth!

As we look through the Bible, we can see that kisses can reveal intentions.

Not every kiss is true love's kiss or a kiss of grace. The most famous kiss in the Bible is Judas' kiss. It was the kiss of betrayal that Satan had worked in his heart.

And while he yet spake, behold a multitude, and he that was called Judas, one of the twelve, went before them, and drew near unto Jesus to kiss him. But Jesus said unto him, Judas, betrayest thou the Son of man with a kiss? Luke 22:47-48

This kiss was meant to be. This did not catch Jesus off guard. He was waiting for it. At the last supper He told Judas.

And after the sop Satan entered into him. Then said Jesus unto him, That thou doest, do quickly. John 13:27

Joseph gave his brothers kisses of forgiveness when he was reunited with them.

And Joseph said unto his brethren, Come near to me, I pray you. And they came near. And he said, I am Joseph your brother, whom ye sold into Egypt. Now therefore be not grieved, nor angry with yourselves, that ye sold me hither: for God did send me before you to preserve life. . .And he fell upon his brother Benjamin's neck, and wept; and Benjamin wept upon his neck. Moreover he kissed all his brethren, and wept upon them: and after that his brethren talked with him. Genesis 45:4-5, 14-15

The father gave the prodigal son kisses of forgiveness.

And he arose, and came to his father. But when he was yet a great way off, his father saw him, and had compassion, and ran, and fell on his neck, and kissed him. Luke 15:20

The woman with the alabaster box gave Jesus the kisses of gratitude. Her many kisses represented her many thanks for all the many sins Jesus forgave her of.

And one of the Pharisees desired him [Jesus] that he would eat with him. And he went into the Pharisee's house, and sat down to meat. And, behold, a woman in the city, which was a sinner, when she knew that Jesus sat at meat in the Pharisee's house, brought an alabaster box of ointment, And stood at his feet behind him weeping, and began to wash his feet with tears, and did wipe them with the hairs of her head, and kissed his feet, and anointed them with the ointment. Now when the Pharisee which had bidden him saw it, he spake within himself, saying, This man, if he were a prophet, would have known who and what manner of woman this is that toucheth him: for she is a sinner. And Jesus answering said unto him, Simon, I have somewhat to say unto thee. And he saith, Master, say on. There was a certain creditor which had two debtors: the one owed five hundred pence, and the other fifty. And when they had nothing to pay, he frankly forgave them both. Tell me therefore, which of them will love him most? Simon answered and said, I suppose that he, to whom he forgave most. And he said unto him,

Thou hast rightly judged. And he turned to the woman, and said unto Simon, Seest thou this woman? I entered into thine house, thou gavest me no water for my feet: but she hath washed my feet with tears, and wiped them with the hairs of her head. Thou gavest me no kiss: but this woman since the time I came in hath not ceased to kiss my feet. My head with oil thou didst not anoint: but this woman hath anointed my feet with ointment. Wherefore I say unto thee, Her sins, which are many, are forgiven; for she loved much: but to whom little is forgiven, the same loveth little. Luke 7:36-47

Then there are the kisses of greeting. When we greet someone with a kiss, it is a gesture of pure intentions. Paul wrote many letters to churches addressing the saints at the beginning of the letters. He often ended his letters encouraging the saints to greet one another with a holy kiss.

Salute one another with an holy kiss. . Romans 16:16

. . .Greet ye one another with an holy kiss. 1 Corinthians 16:20

Greet one another with an holy kiss. 2 Corinthians 13:12

Greet all the brethren with an holy kiss. 1 Thessalonians 5:26

Greet ye one another with a kiss of charity. 1 Peter 5:14

And when our hearts are kissed with God's love-truth it is true love's kiss and everyone of our intentions are revealed.

For the word of God is living and active and sharper than any two-edged sword, and piercing as far as the division of soul and spirit, of both joints and marrow, and able to judge the thoughts and intentions of the heart. Hebrews 4:12 NASB

JESUS CHRIST LIGHT

. . . Worship God in adoring embrace,
Celebrate in trembling awe. Kiss Messiah!
Your very lives are in danger, you know;
His anger is about to explode,
But if you make a run for God—you won't regret it. Psalm 2:10-12 The Message

THE PLEASURES AND THE CHOICES

When we follow pleasure in the Bible, there is usually a choice involved.

The devil is the god of this world, and the work of the devil is sin. The world is filled with sin. Sin is ungodly pleasure and comprised of lusts and pride. Ungodly pleasure is dark, it is selfish, and it is destructive. Jesus came to destroy the works of the devil!

The one who does what is sinful is of the devil, because the devil has been sinning from the beginning. The reason the Son of God appeared was to destroy the devil's work.1 John 3:8 NIV

For all that *is* in the world, the lust of the flesh, and the lust of the eyes, and the pride of life, is not of the Father, but is of the world. 1 John 2:16

When we choose our pleasure over God it is ungodly, and it is sin and it leads to destruction; death.

If we are tempted by such trials, we must not say, "This temptation comes from God." For God cannot be tempted by evil, and he himself tempts no one. But we are tempted when we are drawn away and trapped by our own evil desires. Then our evil desires conceive and give birth to sin; and sin, when it is full-grown, gives birth to death. James 1:13-15 GNT

Eve, the mother of all living, chose her desire for the forbidden fruit over her desire for God. It was ungodly and it was sin and led to destruction; a curse.

Eve was pulled away from God's pleasure to give the first couple, *a beautiful garden filled with every tree pleasant to the sight and good for food* (Genesis 2:7-9) *that they could freely eat of except one* (Genesis 2:16-17) and she was pulled into her own pleasure, *to be as gods, knowing good and evil,* and we all fell for it.

Lot chose to pitch his tent toward Sodom and Gomorrah. The men of Sodom were wicked and sinners before the Lord exceedingly. Lot's choice of land put Lot and his family in a position to see and hear wicked deeds daily.

And Lot lifted up his eyes, and beheld all the plain of Jordan, that it was well watered every where, before the Lord destroyed Sodom and Gomorrah, even as the garden of the Lord, like the land of Egypt, as thou comest unto Zoar. Then Lot chose him all the plain of Jordan; and Lot journeyed east: and they separated themselves the one from the other. Abram dwelled in the land of Canaan, and Lot dwelled in the cities of the plain, and pitched his tent toward Sodom. But the men of Sodom were wicked and sinners before the Lord exceedingly. Genesis 13:10-13

God sent two angels to pull Lot and his daughters out of that, but his wife and son in laws were destroyed.

And Lot went out, and spake unto his sons in law, which married his daughters, and said, Up, get you out of this place; for the LORD will destroy this city. But he seemed as one that mocked unto his sons in law. And when the morning arose, then the angels hastened Lot, saying, Arise, take thy wife, and thy two daughters, which are here; lest thou be consumed in the iniquity of the city. And while he lingered, the men laid hold upon his hand, and upon the hand of his wife, and upon the hand of his two daughters; the LORD being merciful unto him: and they brought him forth, and set him without the city. Genesis 19:14-16

But his wife looked back from behind him, and she became a pillar of salt. Genesis 19:26

And delivered just Lot, vexed with the filthy conversation of the wicked: (For that righteous man dwelling among them, in seeing and hearing, vexed his righteous soul from day to day with their unlawful deeds;) 2 Peter 2:7-8

Solomon's choice for wisdom to judge God's people over fame and fortune was godly and it was right. It made him the wisest king ever, enriching the lives of God's people.

And now, O LORD my God, thou hast made thy servant king instead of David my father: and I am but a little child: I know not how to go out or come in. And thy servant is in the midst of thy people which thou hast chosen, a great people, that cannot be numbered nor counted for multitude. Give therefore thy servant an understanding heart to judge thy people, that I may discern between good and bad: for who is able to judge this thy so great a people? And the speech pleased the LORD, that Solomon had asked this thing. And God said unto him, Because thou hast asked this thing, and hast not asked for thyself long life; neither hast asked riches for thyself, nor hast asked the life of thine enemies; but hast asked for thyself understanding to discern judgment; Behold, I have done according to thy words: lo, I have given thee a wise and an understanding heart; so that there was none like thee before thee, neither after thee shall any arise like unto thee. 1 Kings 3:7-12

Moses' choice to please God more than to please himself with the pleasures in Egypt was godly and it was right and eventually brought deliverance to God's people.

By faith Moses, when he was come to years, refused to be called the son of Pharaoh's daughter; Choosing rather to suffer affliction with the people of God, than to enjoy the pleasures of sin for a season; Esteeming the reproach of Christ greater riches than the treasures in Egypt: for he had respect unto the recompence of the reward. By faith he forsook Egypt, not fearing the wrath of the king: for he endured, as seeing him who is invisible. Hebrews 11:24-27

Jesus told a parable about how choosing the pleasures of this life over God is ungodly and it is sin and can stop the work of God's word in our lives.

Now the parable is this: The seed is the word of God. . .And that which fell among thorns are they, which, when they have heard, go forth, and are choked with cares and riches and pleasures of this life, and bring no fruit to perfection. . . Read entire parable Luke 8:11-15

Paul wrote to Timothy to not have anything to do with ungodly and sinful people who choose themselves over God.

But mark this: There will be terrible times in the last days. People will be lovers of themselves, lovers of money, boastful, proud, abusive, disobedient to their parents, ungrateful, unholy, without love, unforgiving, slanderous, without self-control, brutal, not lovers of the good, treacherous, rash, conceited, lovers of pleasure rather than lovers of God— having a form of godliness but denying its power. Have nothing to do with such people. 2 Timothy 3:1-5 NIV

We were born into this world through no choice of our own, and as a sinner at that, but from our very first breath, we have opportunities to choose God over sin. Every time we hear God's love-truth, the gospel of Jesus Christ, we have an opportunity to choose God over sin. And that's the God's absolute love-truth!

For the grace of God has been revealed, bringing salvation to all people. And we are instructed to turn from godless living and sinful pleasures. We should live in this evil world with wisdom, righteousness, and devotion to God, while we look forward with hope to that wonderful day when the glory of our great God and Savior, Jesus Christ, will be revealed. He gave his life to free us from every kind of sin, to cleanse us, and to make us his very own people, totally committed to doing good deeds. Titus 2:11-14 NLT

JESUS CHRIST LIGHT

Fear not, little flock; for it is your Father's good pleasure to give you the kingdom. Luke 12:32

THE FOLLOW AND THE END

In this age of social media, we follow people and people follow us. And we usually follow whoever we find inspiring or who we can relate to, and our hearts dictate that. We must realize that when we follow someone, they are leading us somewhere. When we follow follow in the Bible, we can see how people are led to a good end or to a bad end.

Adam and Eve should have kept following God to eternal life, but Eve followed the serpent to a curse. She was sentenced to hard labor.

Unto the woman he said, I will greatly multiply thy sorrow and thy conception; in sorrow thou shalt bring forth children; and thy desire shall be to thy husband, and he shall rule over thee. Genesis 3:16

And Adam followed Eve to the curse. He too, was sentenced to hard labor.

And unto Adam he said, Because thou hast hearkened unto the voice of thy wife, and hast eaten of the tree, of which I commanded thee, saying, Thou shalt not eat of it: cursed is the ground for thy sake; in sorrow shalt thou eat of it all the days of thy life; Thorns also and thistles shall it bring forth to thee; and thou shalt eat the herb of the field; In the sweat of thy face shalt thou eat bread, till thou return unto the ground; for out of it wast thou taken: for dust thou art, and unto dust shalt thou return. Genesis 3:17-19

And of course, they would both eventually die because of the tree. Before Christ, we follow Adam.

For as in Adam all die. . . 1 Corinthians 15:22

For when ye were the servants of sin, ye were free from righteousness. What fruit had ye then in those things whereof ye are now ashamed? for the end of those things is death. Romans 6:20-21

They followed righteous Noah into the ark and ended up in a good dry place. The world of the ungodly didn't follow Noah and ended up in the great flood.

In the selfsame day entered Noah, and Shem, and Ham, and Japheth, the sons of Noah, and Noah's wife, and the three wives of his sons with them, into the ark; They, and every beast after his kind, and all the cattle after their kind, and every creeping thing that creepeth upon the earth after his kind, and every fowl after his kind, every bird of every sort. And they went in unto Noah into the ark, two and two of all flesh, wherein is the breath of life. And they that went in, went in male and female of all flesh, as God had commanded him: and the LORD shut him in. Genesis 7:13-16

Those that followed the preacher of righteousness into the ark were saved, those that didn't follow the flood was brought on them.

And spared not the old world, but saved Noah the eighth *person*, a preacher of righteousness, bringing in the flood upon the world of the ungodly; 2 Peter 2:5

The children of Israel followed faithful Moses out of the land of bricks and mortar into a land flowing with milk and honey.

And I am come down to deliver them out of the hand of the Egyptians, and to bring them up out of that land unto a good land and a large, unto a land flowing with milk and honey; unto the place of the Canaanites, and the Hittites, and the Amorites, and the Perizzites, and the Hivites, and the Jebusites. Now therefore, behold, the cry of the children of Israel is come unto me: and I have also seen the oppression wherewith the Egyptians oppress them. Come now therefore, and I will send thee unto Pharaoh, that thou mayest bring forth my people the children of Israel out of Egypt. Exodus 3:8-10

People were following the God's messenger John the Baptist. He was preaching repentance and baptizing people in the river Jordan.

Then went out to him Jerusalem, and all Judaea, and all the region round about Jordan, And were baptized of him in Jordan, confessing their sins. Matthew 3:5-6

These people that followed John the Baptist were led to the Lamb of God. When John the Baptist saw Jesus coming to be baptized by him, he cried out who He was.

The next day John seeth Jesus coming unto him, and saith, Behold the Lamb of God, which taketh away the sin of the world. John 1:29

People began following Jesus Christ to many wonderful things.

To fish for souls

And he saith unto them, Follow me, and I will make you fishers of men. Matthew 4:19

To the light of life.

Then spake Jesus again unto them, saying, I am the light of the world: he that followeth me shall not walk in darkness, but shall have the light of life. John 8:12

Eternal life

. . .in Christ shall all be made alive. 1 Corinthians 15:22

. . .the gift of God is eternal life through Jesus Christ our Lord. Romans 6:22-23

The Word of God

All Scripture is given by inspiration of God, and is profitable for doctrine, for reproof, for correction, for instruction in righteousness, that the man of God may be complete, thoroughly equipped for every good work. 2 Timothy 3:16-17 NKJV

JESUS CHRIST LIGHT

Jesus told his disciples

If any *man* will come after me, let him deny himself, and take up his cross, and follow me. Matthew 16:24

APPLYING GOD'S LOVE-TRUTH AND THE REBIRTH

God's love-truth doesn't mean anything to an unbeliever. When the Pharaoh that Moses confronted heard the word of God, he did not believe. Faith did not come. He is a prime example of a hard heart. He did not know the Lord. He did not believe the Lord. God's word meant nothing to him.

When he heard God's command, his response was, *Who is the LORD, that I should obey his voice?*

And afterward Moses and Aaron went in, and told Pharaoh, Thus saith the LORD God of Israel, Let my people go, that they may hold a feast unto me in the wilderness. And Pharaoh said, Who is the LORD, that I should obey his voice to let Israel go? I know not the LORD, neither will I let Israel go. Exodus 5:1-2

The Bible says we are all sinners and need saving, and we must admit to that. That is hard thing for some people to admit to especially in this day and age.

For everyone has sinned; we all fall short of God's glorious standard. Yet God, in his grace, freely makes us right in his sight. He did this through Christ Jesus when he freed us from the penalty for our sins. For God presented Jesus as the sacrifice for sin. People are made right with God when they believe that Jesus sacrificed his life, shedding his blood. This sacrifice shows that God was being fair when he held back and did not punish those who sinned in times past, for he was looking ahead and including them in what he would do in this present time. God did this to demonstrate his righteousness, for he himself is fair and just, and he makes sinners right in his sight when they believe in Jesus. Romans 3:23-26 NLT

And we must believe the Word of God about the righteousness of Christ.

For he hath made him to be sin for us, who knew no sin; that we might be made the righteousness of God in him. 2 Corinthians 5:21

And we must believe the word of God about rebirth by believing on Jesus.

Jesus told Nicodemus.

That which is born of the flesh is flesh; and that which is born of the Spirit is spirit. Marvel not that I said unto thee, Ye must be born again. . .And as Moses lifted up the serpent in the wilderness, even so must the Son of man be lifted up: That whosoever believeth in him should not perish, but have eternal life. For God so loved the world, that he gave his only begotten Son, that whosoever believeth in him should not perish, but have everlasting life. For God sent not his Son into the world to condemn the world; but that the world through him might be saved. John 3:6-7; 14-17

Born again work is God's work in our hearts. It is salvation! It is spiritual and it is powerful and it is life changing! He has given us His Word and His Spirit. God does the saving work, we do the believing. He will wash away our sins and give us new and eternal life.

Once we, too, were foolish and disobedient. We were misled and became slaves to many lusts and pleasures. Our lives were full of evil and envy, and we hated each other. But when God our Savior revealed his kindness and love, he saved us, not because of the righteous things we had done, but because of his mercy. He washed away our sins, giving us a new birth and new life through the Holy Spirit. He generously poured out the Spirit upon us through Jesus Christ our Savior. Because of his grace he made us right in his sight and gave us confidence that we will inherit eternal life. Titus 3:3-7 NLT

We can be born again when we believe Jesus died for our sins, He was buried and He rose again the third day all according to Scriptures.

For I delivered unto you first of all that which I also received, how that Christ died for our sins according to the scriptures; And that he was buried, and that he rose again the third day according to the scriptures: And that he was seen of Cephas, then of the twelve: After that, he was seen of above five hundred brethren at once; of whom the greater part remain unto this present, but some are fallen asleep. After that, he was seen of James; then of all the apostles. And last of all he was seen of me also, as of one born out of due time. 1 Corinthians 15:3-8

To rise again is to become alive again. To be born again is to die to our old life and be born anew.

Peter wrote.

Being born again, not of corruptible seed, but of incorruptible, by the word of God, which liveth and abideth for ever. 1 Peter 1:23

Paul wrote.

I am crucified with Christ: nevertheless I live; yet not I, but Christ liveth in me: and the life which I now live in the flesh I live by the faith of the Son of God, who loved me, and gave himself for me. Galatians 2:20

And this born again experience is for Jews and Gentiles.

Paul wrote.

...So I ask, "Has Israel stumbled so badly that it can't get up again?" That's unthinkable! By Israel's failure, salvation has come to people who are not Jewish to make the Jewish people jealous. The fall of the Jewish people made the world spiritually rich. Their failure made people who are not Jewish spiritually rich. So, the inclusion of Jewish people will make the world even richer. Romans 11:11-12 GW

And as we walk out this new life in Christ, we walk it out by knowing and obeying all God's love-truths in the Bible.

...If ye continue in my word, then are ye my disciples indeed; And ye shall know the truth, and the truth shall make you free. John 8:28-32

We know we are born again because God says,

For whosoever shall call upon the name of the Lord shall be saved...So then faith cometh by hearing, and hearing by the word of God. Romans 10:13,17

Evidence of this new rebirth is seen in our love for our brothers and sisters in Christ, and in our desire to live right.

So now we can tell who are children of God and who are children of the devil. Anyone who does not live righteously and does not love other believers does not belong to God. 1 John 3:10 NLT

JESUS CHRIST LIGHT

Think for a moment about the person who you can trust with all your heart and why that is. Trusting is believing someone loves us and wants what is best for us and will move heaven and earth to help us. They will defend us and will never, ever lie to us. We ask those people into our hearts.

There is plenty of Scripture that backs up having Christ in our hearts.

And because ye are sons, God hath sent forth the Spirit of his Son into your hearts, crying, Abba, Father. Galatians 4:6

That Christ may dwell in your hearts by faith; that ye, being rooted and grounded in love,

May be able to comprehend with all saints what is the breadth, and length, and depth, and height; And to know the love of Christ, which passeth knowledge, that ye might be filled with all the fulness of God. . . Ephesians 3:17-21

So, we ask Jesus to come into our hearts by praying a prayer. We call on His Name. We confess that He alone is our righteousness and our only way to our Father in heaven.

If you confess with your mouth the Lord Jesus and believe in your heart that God has raised Him from the dead, you will be saved. For with the heart one believes unto righteousness, and with the mouth confession is made unto salvation. Romans 10:9-10 NKJV

Heartfelt Prayer

Our prayer could be like wedding vows.

"I, (fill in your name) take You, Lord Jesus Christ as my Lord and Savior. You are the only way to my Father in heaven because You alone are righteous. I believe you died for my sins, was buried and rose again from the dead to save me from my sins and give me eternal life! I believe You have power on earth to forgive sins, so please forgive me of all my sins. Baptize me with Your Holy Spirit and Your love. Amen

The day we call upon the Name of the Lord Jesus Christ to save us is the day we begin a personal relationship with Father, Son and Holy Spirit. And this is the God's absolute love-truth!

Therefore if any man be in Christ, he is a new creature: old things are passed away; behold, all things are become new. And all things are of God, who hath reconciled us to himself by Jesus Christ, and hath given to us the ministry of reconciliation; 2 Corinthians 5:17-18

So, if you just prayed that prayer, you could really begin to understand God's love-truth; God's absolute love-truth! So, go back and read this little book again, and it should be even clearer than it was before because,

. . .No one can know a person's thoughts except that person's own spirit, and no one can know God's thoughts except God's own Spirit. And we have received God's Spirit (not the world's spirit), so we can know the wonderful things God has freely given us. . . 1Corinthians 2:9-14 NLT

And absolutely read the Holy Bible every day of your life for it is filled to the brim with God's love-truth and it's on God's love-truth that we stand.

And pray!

And get with other Christians!

And find a good church and community!

KNOWLEDGE OF GOOD AND EVIL

In the Garden of Eden there was the tree of the knowledge of good and evil and that was the one tree God told Adam and Eve not to eat of, yet they ate of it. I think we should know the difference between good and evil for that keeps us safe, but for some reason God banned Adam and Eve from that tree. God is good, so the knowledge of good comes from God. The devil is evil. *Could the knowledge of evil come from him?*

Beloved, follow not that which is evil, but that which is good. He that doeth good is of God: but he that doeth evil hath not seen God. 3 John 1:11

We can see the effects evil has had on our world today. There are way too many people who are way too familiar with evil.

Paul wrote,

. . .I want you to be wise in doing right and to stay innocent of any wrong. Romans 16:19 NLT

In this chapter, we are going to look at why evil is not good. We all know the obvious reasons evil is not good but let's look into God's word at the not so obvious reasons evil is not good. I'm not going to try and explain all the reasons I'm listing; I'm just going to list the Scriptures.

Evil banned mankind from the Tree of Life.

And the Lord God said, Behold, the man is become as one of us, to know good and evil: and now, lest he put forth his hand, and take also of the tree of life, and eat, and live for ever: Genesis 3:22

Evil brought about the great flood.

And God saw that the wickedness of man was great in the earth, and that every imagination of the thoughts of his heart was only evil continually. And it repented the LORD that he had made man on the earth, and it grieved him at his heart. And the LORD said, I will destroy man whom I have created from the face of the earth; both man, and beast, and the creeping thing, and the fowls of the air; for it repenteth me that I have made them. Genesis 6:5-7

Evil is God-less.

For thou art not a God that hath pleasure in wickedness: neither shall evil dwell with thee. Psalm 5:4

Evil will be forgotten.

The face of the Lord is against them that do evil, to cut off the remembrance of them from the earth. Psalm 34:16

Evil will be cut down and wither.

Fret not thyself because of evildoers, neither be thou envious against the workers of iniquity. For they shall soon be cut down like the grass, and wither as the green herb. Psalm 37:1-2

Evil is deceptive.

Deceit is in the heart of them that imagine evil:. . .Proverbs 12:20

Evil pursues sinners. . .Proverbs 13:21

The evil bow before the good;. . .Proverbs 14:19

Evil is error.

Do they not err that devise evil?. . .Proverbs 14:22

Evil is rebellion.

An evil man seeketh only rebellion:. . .Proverbs 17:11

Evil is punished.

A prudent man foreseeth the evil, and hideth himself: but the simple pass on, and are punished. Proverbs 22:3

Evil has no reward.

For there shall be no reward to the evil man ; the candle of the wicked shall be put out. Proverbs 24:20

Evil is unjust.

Evil men understand not judgment:. . .Proverbs 28:5

Evil will fall.

Whoso causeth the righteous to go astray in an evil way, he shall fall himself into his own pit: Proverbs 28:10

Evil is a trap.

In the transgression of an evil man there is a snare:. . .Proverbs 29:6

Evil is dark.

For every one that doeth evil hateth the light, neither cometh to the light, lest his deeds should be reproved. John 3:20

Evil is damned.

And shall come forth; they that have done good, unto the resurrection of life; and they that have done evil, unto the resurrection of damnation. John 5:29

Evil is punished

Tribulation and anguish, upon every soul of man that doeth evil, of the Jew first, and also of the Gentile; Romans 2:9

Evil is sorrow

For the love of money is the root of all evil: which while some coveted after, they have erred from the faith, and pierced themselves through with many sorrows. 1 Timothy 6:10

Here is a Scripture from Hosea about the Lord having a controversy with the people because there was no truth, no mercy, no knowledge of God in the land. The land suffered because of evil.

Hear the word of the Lord, ye children of Israel: for the Lord hath a controversy with the inhabitants of the land, because there is no truth, nor mercy, nor knowledge of God in the land. By swearing, and lying, and killing, and stealing, and committing adultery, they break out, and blood toucheth blood. Therefore shall the land mourn, and every one that dwelleth therein shall languish, with the beasts of the field, and with the fowls of heaven; yea, the fishes of the sea also shall be taken away. Yet let no man strive, nor reprove another: for thy people are as they that strive with the priest. Therefore shalt thou fall in the day, and the prophet also shall fall with thee in the night, and I will destroy thy mother. My people are destroyed for lack of knowledge: because thou hast rejected knowledge, I will also reject thee, that thou shalt be no priest to me: seeing thou hast forgotten the law of thy God, I will also forget thy children. Hosea 4:1-6

There are many religions in the world. Christianity is not a religion. It is a relationship. It is a fellowship. It is a family. People serve many 'gods' but those 'gods' are not a Father God. The God, who in the beginning created the heavens, the earth, the seas and all things therein, wants us to know Him as our Father. Knowing God as our Father is good to know.

Here are some Scriptures about knowing, our Father.

Our Father is in heaven! Yes, there is a heaven! We pray. . .

. . .Our Father which art in heaven. . .Matthew 6:9

We come to know God as our Father by knowing Jesus.

Then said they unto him, Where is thy Father? Jesus answered, Ye neither know me, nor my Father: if ye had known me, ye should have known my Father also. John 8:19

In our Father's house there are many mansions.

In my Father's house are many mansions: if it were not so, I would have told you. I go to prepare a place for you. John 14:2

Our Father sends us comfort, even the Spirit of truth.

And I will pray the Father, and he shall give you another Comforter, that he may abide with you for ever; Even the Spirit of truth; whom the world cannot receive, because it seeth him not, neither knoweth him: but ye know him; for he dwelleth with you, and shall be in you. John 14:16-17

Jesus loves us with the same love His Father loves Him with.

As the Father hath loved me, so have I loved you: continue ye in my love. John 15:9

Jesus prayer for oneness.

Neither pray I for these alone, but for them also which shall believe on me through their word; That they all may be one; as thou, Father, art in me, and I in thee, that they also may be one in us: that the world may believe that thou hast sent me. John 17:20-21

All things work together for our good.

And we know that all things work together for good to them that love God, to them who are the called according to his purpose. For whom he did foreknow, he also did predestinate to be conformed to the image of his Son, that he might be the firstborn among many brethren.

Moreover whom he did predestinate, them he also called: and whom he called, them he also justified: and whom he justified, them he also glorified. What shall we then say to these things? If God be for us, who can be against us? He that spared not his own Son, but delivered him up for us all, how shall he not with him also freely give us all things? Romans 8:28-32

Our Father is the Father of mercies and the God of all comfort.

Blessed be God, even the Father of our Lord Jesus Christ, the Father of mercies, and the God of all comfort; Who comforteth us in all our tribulation, that we may be able to comfort them which are in any trouble, by the comfort wherewith we ourselves are comforted of God. 2 Corinthians 1:3-4

We cry out Abba Father as sons and daughters

And because ye are sons, God hath sent forth the Spirit of his Son into your hearts, crying, Abba, Father. Wherefore thou art no more a servant, but a son; and if a son, then an heir of God through Christ. Galatians 4:6-7

Our Father gives to us the spirit of wisdom and revelation.

That the God of our Lord Jesus Christ, the Father of glory, may give unto you the spirit of wisdom and revelation in the knowledge of him: The eyes of your understanding being enlightened; that ye may know what is the hope of his calling, and what the riches of the glory of his inheritance in the saints, And what is the exceeding greatness of his power to us-ward who believe, according to the working of his mighty power, Which he wrought in Christ, when he raised him from the dead, and set him at his own right hand in the heavenly places, Far above all principality, and power, and might, and dominion, and every name that is named, not only in this world, but also in that which is to come: And hath put all things under his feet, and gave him to be the head over all things to the church, Which is his body, the fulness of him that filleth all in all. Ephesians 1:17-23

Our Father makes us partakers of the inheritance of the saints in light and delivers us from the power of darkness.

Giving thanks unto the Father, which hath made us meet to be partakers of the inheritance of the saints in light: Who hath delivered us from the power of darkness, and hath translated us into the kingdom of his dear Son: Colossians 1:12-13

Our Father has given us everlasting consolation and good hope.

Now our Lord Jesus Christ himself, and God, even our Father, which hath loved us, and hath given us everlasting consolation and good hope through grace, Comfort your hearts, and stablish you in every good word and work. 2 Thessalonians 2:16-17

Every good and perfect gift comes down from Our Father.

Every good gift and every perfect gift is from above, and cometh down from the Father of lights, with whom is no variableness, neither shadow of turning. Of his own will begat he us with the word of truth, that we should be a kind of firstfruits of his creatures. James 1:17-18

Our fellowship is with our Father and His Son and one another.

(For the life was manifested, and we have seen it, and bear witness, and shew unto you that eternal life, which was with the Father, and was manifested unto us;) That which we have seen and heard declare we unto you, that ye also may have fellowship with us: and truly our fellowship is with the Father, and with his Son Jesus Christ.1 John 1:2-3

Our Father sent His Son to save us.

And we have seen and do testify that the Father sent the Son to be the Saviour of the world. 1 John 4:14

Our Father bears record in heaven.

Who is he that overcometh the world, but he that believeth that Jesus is the Son of God? This is he that came by water and blood, even Jesus Christ; not by water only, but by water and blood. And it is the Spirit that beareth witness, because the Spirit is truth. For there are three that bear record in heaven, the Father, the Word, and the Holy Ghost: and these three are one. And there are three that bear witness in earth, the Spirit, and the water, and the blood: and these three agree in one.1 John 5:5-8

Jesus has made us kings and priests unto His Father.

And from Jesus Christ, who is the faithful witness, and the first begotten of the dead, and the prince of the kings of the earth. Unto him that loved us, and washed us from our sins in his own blood, And hath made us kings and priests unto God and his Father; to him be glory and dominion for ever and ever. Amen. Revelation 1:5-6

JESUS CHRIST LIGHT

Jesus saith unto him, I am the way, the truth, and the life: no man cometh unto the Father, but by me. John 14:6

THE HEART AND GOD'S LOVE-TRUTH

Hearts that hold God's love-truth hold infinite treasures. This last chapter is all about hearts that hold God's love-truth. It starts out with a poem and ends with a list of things our hearts can do.

Like the fathomless sea, our hearts are deep. Thoughts like sea creatures swim and creep. Wishes fly round and we hope things get better. If faith is aroused, dark days can get brighter. Sharp words pierce through bringing many sorrows. Leaving us broken and dreading tomorrow. If bitter branches are allowed to take root, all that will spring forth is dried up old fruit. Our hearts, like candles can certainly melt at cry of baby or when a sad song is felt. We're made soft because beauty has touched us, or perhaps because we've met up with sadness. All we love is held in reverence there, along with our fears, prayers and cares. God in the heavens is well aware of these, the things we dream and things we think. At heart's very core where we believe, lay hidden treasure at God's heartbeat. His heart pumps Words that give life, bringing peace and warding off the strife.

Our hearts are amazing!

Now, here is a long list, not an exhausted study, of all our hearts can hold. Read it all the way through first, then when you have time, read the Scriptures and text surrounding the Scriptures for a clearer understanding of what our hearts hold. And as you notice the transition from negative to positive, think about how our hearts can be transformed by holding within them, God's love-truth!

OUR HEARTS CAN

Have sorrow Psalms 13:2
Hold troubles Psalms 25:17
Plan evil Psalms 28:3
Work wickedness Psalms 58:2
Gather iniquity Psalms 41:6
Turn back Psalms 44:18
Have war Psalms 55:21
Be stout Psalms 76:5
Tempt God Psalms 78:18
Hold lusts Psalms 81:12
Be hardened Psalms 95:8
Err Psalms 95:10
Be smitten Psalms 102:4
Be oppressed Psalms 107:12
Be wounded Psalms 109:22
Be desolate Psalms 143:4
Hate reproof Proverbs 5:12
Be sly Proverbs 7:10
Be perverse Proverbs 12:8
Hold deceit Proverbs 12:20
Proclaim foolishness Proverbs 12:23
Be heavy Proverbs 12:25
Be bitter Proverbs 14:10
Be backslidden Proverbs 14:14
Devise its way Proverbs 16:9
Fret against the Lord Proverbs 19:3
Hold foolishness Proverbs 22:15
Envy sinners Proverbs 23:17
Hold betrayal John 13:2
Conceive a lie Acts 5:3
Utter perverse things Proverbs 23:33
Study destruction Proverbs 24:2
Hold abominations Proverbs 26:25

Be not right with God Acts 8:21
Be dark Romans 1:21
Be impenitent Romans 2:5
Have a veil upon it 2 Corinthians 3:15
Hold evil and unbelief Hebrews 3:12
Be deceived James 1:26
Have bitter envying and strife James 3:14
Be covetous 2 Peter 2:14
Have turmoil Psalms 38:8
Condemn us 1 John 3:20
Fail Psalms 40:12

Be single minded Acts 2:46
Be impressed Acts 7:23
Understand John 12:40
Be perfect Psalms 101:2
Be wise Proverbs 10:8
Hold gladness Psalms 4:7
Be tried Psalms 7:9
Praise God Psalms 9:1
Speak Psalms 10:6
Rejoice Psalms 13:5
Meditate Psalms 19:14
Be pure Psalms 24:4
Be strengthened Psalms 27:14
Trust Psalms 28:7
Be upright Psalms 32:11
Be fashioned Psalms 33:15
Hold God's laws Psalms 37:31
Hold secrets Psalms 44:21
Indite a good matter Psalms 45:1
Be created clean Psalm 51:10
Be broken and contrite Psalms 51:17
Be fixed Psalms 57:7
Be overwhelmed Psalms 61:2

Be deep Psalms 64:6
Live Psalms 69:32
Wish Psalms 73:7
Grieve Psalms 73:21
Cry out to God Psalms 84:2
Be established Psalms 112:8
Seek Psalms 119:2
Have God's Word hidden there Psalms 119:11
Be enlarged Psalms 119:32
Be inclined to God's Word Psalms 119:36
Keep God's precepts Psalms 119:69
Have awe of God's Word Psalms 119:161
Apply understanding Proverbs 2:2
Keep God's commandments Proverbs 3:1
Be written upon Proverbs 3:3
Retain God's words Proverbs 4:4
Spring forth the issues of life Proverbs 4:23
Be merry Proverbs 15:13
Study to answer Proverbs 15:28
Hold counsel Proverbs 20:5
Be turned by God Proverbs 21:1
Be weighed by God Proverbs 21:2
Be guided Proverbs 23:19
Have purpose Acts 11:23
Be purified Acts 15:9
Be opened Acts 16:14
Have God's love in them Romans 5:5
Be obedient Romans 6:17
Have God's Word in them Romans 10:8
Believe unto righteousness Romans 10:10
Stand steadfast 1 Corinthians 7:37
Be sealed with God's Spirit 2 Corinthians 1:22
Have God's light 2 Corinthians 4:6
Have the Spirit of God's Son Galatians 4:6
Have Christ live there Ephesians 3:17

Be tender Ephesians 4:32
Do God's will Ephesians 6:6
Be comforted Ephesians 6:22
Hold people Philippians 1:7
Be guarded by peace Philippians 4:7
Be knit together in love Colossians 2:2
Be ruled by God's peace Colossians 3:15
Be directed into God's love 2 Thessalonians 3:5
Have intents Hebrews 4:12
Draw near to God Hebrews 10:22
Be established with grace Hebrews 13:9
Be nourished James 5:5
Be meek and quiet 1 Peter 3:4
Condemn us not 1 John 3:21
END

www.ingramcontent.com/pod-product-compliance
Lightning Source LLC
Chambersburg PA
CBHW020447220526
45464CB00002B/893